# THE COMPLETE GUIDE TO PIT BULLS

Erin Hotovy

LP Media Inc. Publishing

Text copyright © 2019 by LP Media Inc.

www.lpmedia.org

Publication Data

Erin, Hotovy.

The Complete Guide to Pit Bulls / Erin Hotovy. ---- First edition.

Summary: "Successfully raising a Pit Bull dog from puppy to old age" --- Provided by publisher.

ISBN: 978-179-468262-7

[1. Pit Bulls --- Non-Fiction] I. Title.

This book has been written with the published intent to provide accurate and author-itative information in regard to the subject matter included. While every reasonable pre-caution has been taken in preparation of this book the author and publisher expressly dis-claim responsibility for any errors, omissions, or adverse effects arising from the use or application of the information contained inside. The techniques and suggestions are to be used at the reader's discretion and are not to be considered a substitute for professional veterinary care. If you suspect a medical problem with your dog, consult your veterinarian.

Design by Sorin Rădulescu

First paperback edition, 2019

# TABLE OF CONTENTS

# THE COMPLETE GUIDE TO PIT BULLS

Pit Bulls are sweet, adorable dogs with a fascinating back story. These dogs have had many different purposes over the years, but are best known today as excellent family dogs. The Pit Bull is not just one breed, but a variety of closely linked breeds that share similar traits. These breeds are often misunderstood due to poor breeding and training practices, but this is not the dog's fault. When bred and raised properly, the Pit Bull is an excellent companion to you and your family.

With any new dog breed, there is a learning curve to take into account. Even if you've owned another dog before, each breed has its own quirks and unique requirements. This book will guide you through the early days of life with your dog, all the way to the very end. You will learn how to find the perfect Pit Bull for you, how to train your new puppy, and even how to travel with your dog. By the end, you will have the information you need to feel confident in your ability to give your Pit Bull the very best life he could ever want!

# CHAPTER 1
# Introduction to Pit Bulls

## What Is a Pit Bull?

This is not necessarily an easy question to answer! The fact is, there are a lot of things a Pit Bull can be. The designation "Pit Bull" often refers to a few different breeds with similarities. This can include the American Staffordshire Terrier, the American Bully, the American Pit Bull Terrier, or a mix of any of those breeds. You can probably recognize these dogs by their short, stocky physique and short snout, though you might have a hard time distinguishing one from another. For the purpose of this book, the name "Pit Bull" will be used when describing any dogs related to the above breeds.

Photo Courtesy of
Luisa Tapia

# History of the Pit Bull

The early Pit Bulls were a crossbreed, bred from bulldogs and terriers. This resulted in a dog that was quick and agile, but also very muscular. In the United Kingdom, these dogs were unfortunately bred to participate in dangerous sports. Bull-baiting was a barbaric sporting event where dogs were used to attack or control an angry bull. The dog was bred to bite a bull's snout, while the bull often thwarted the dog's attempts by launching it into the air. This sport was also practiced with bears instead of bulls, which forced the dog to fight an angry bear. However, this sport was prohibited in 1835, as it was cruel to the animals involved.

## FUN FACT
### What is a Pit Bull?

"Pit bull" is an umbrella term for many breeds including the American Staffordshire Terrier, American Pit Bull Terrier, and Staffordshire Bull Terrier. Initially they were bred from Old English bulldogs for bullfighting. After this, pit bulls were typically known as working dogs until people began using them for dogfighting. News media has unfairly stigmatized pit bulls based on fear and generalization. Every pit bull's demeanor is determined by how the dog is treated, trained, and cared for.

Unfortunately, this did not keep the breed safe. Instead, people went from large, public fighting events to smaller, more private venues. Because these spaces were smaller, dogs were made to fight other dogs. While this practice has long been illegal, Pit Bulls are still occasionally used for this purpose today. Though these dogs were purposefully bred to be fierce fighters, they were specifically bred not to bite humans—only other animals.

Despite their unfortunate past, this breed has taken on a new appreciation as a family pet. These dogs were even used to move livestock because of their determination and strength. They came to America with their British immigrant owners and have found a home here in the United States. Now, they are often referred to as "nanny dogs" because of how well they get along with kids.

# Different Breeds Within the Pit Bull Designation

When talking about the Pit Bull, there are a few different dog breeds that you may encounter. For the most part, these are all variations of the original Pit Bull, but there are still some noticeable differences.

While there are many different crossbreeds when it comes to Pit Bulls, here are a few common breeds you'll see. The American Pit Bull Terrier has slightly longer legs and is not nearly as stout as other kinds of Pit Bulls. This is the only Pit Bull breed that is recognized by the United Kennel Club and American Dog Breeders Association. The American Staffordshire Terrier is a little bulkier and has a square-shaped body. The Staffordshire Bull Terrier is smaller and has a broad head and rounded body.

Some breeds are often confused for Pit Bulls because of their bulky bodies. While American Bulldogs, Boxers, and Bull Terriers are all short and stocky dogs, they are not considered to be part of the Pit Bull family.

*American Pit Bull Terrier*

*American Staffordshire Terrier*

*Staffordshire Bull Terrier*

*Photo Courtesy of Sharna Wood*

# Physical Characteristics

While there is no standard for this mix of breeds, you'll find that most Pit Bulls share a set of physical characteristics. Most notable is their muscular build. While they don't grow up to be much larger than twenty inches high or so, they can weigh anywhere from thirty to seventy pounds, depending on their bloodline. They also have an easily distinguishable head shape that's broad and flat. Their tail is usually pointed and wagging wildly; however, some owners choose to dock their Pit Bull's tail. This is often the case in dogs that are used for fighting, so there might be a greater proportion of tailless dogs in shelters. This applies to Pit Bulls with cropped ears as well. You'll also find Pit Bulls' eyes are often set far apart on their broad head.

These dogs have a very short and smooth coat. For the most part, this coat is straight and their fur is coarse. Pit Bulls can come in a variety of colors. Brown, white, black, red, and fawn are all common coat colors for this breed. These dogs can also be a combination of several colors. Though the single coat sheds, grooming is incredibly easy.

11

# Behavioral Characteristics

*"Temperament is the most important attribute, especially when dealing with a family dog or a dog used for working. You have to know what you're buying in an American Pitbull Terrier or an American Bully. Both breeds look similar but are very different dogs when it comes to personality and function."*

**James Jackson**
*Flatline Kennels*

At its core, the Pit Bull is a companion animal. These dogs love to spend as much time as possible with their humans. In fact, these dogs truly hate to be left alone for extended periods of time. They want to play and follow you around the house. These dogs should not be kept outside all the time because they would miss out on valuable family time.

These dogs are also known for being great with children. They are gentle around kids and love to play with them. They are also generally good with strangers. While your Pit Bull's loyalty may make them a little cautious when you open your home to strangers, they'll soon warm up to anyone they meet. This dog just wants to have all of the love and attention they can get. This dog is very social with people, so they're a great addition to a full house. The Pit Bull is not an effective guard dog because they're much more likely to lick an intruder than scare them away with meanness.

This breed can be less friendly with other animals. It's possible to have a Pit Bull and other pets in your home, but make sure they are well socialized with other animals first. Or, if you don't already have pets, you may decide that this Pit Bull will be an only pet. Nevertheless, it is important to have your Pit Bull interact with other dogs to develop the skills they need to be a good canine citizen.

Pit Bulls are also smart and capable of learning a wide variety of tricks and skills. Training can be a lot of fun with this breed because they are sensitive and aim to please. They will enjoy the interactive time with their owner and it will keep them entertained. It's also a good idea to master a few key obedience skills so if strangers are nervous around your dog, you can show them that they have nothing to fear.

# Myths and Controversies

Pit Bulls get a bad reputation from the humans who have misused the breed. It's not their fault they have a strong, intimidating body. When bred and handled incorrectly, any dog has the ability to be dangerous. Pit Bulls just get a worse reputation because their breed has been used for fighting. Local governments perpetuate this negative stereotype by creating muzzle rules for public spaces, or even banning the breeds altogether!

One misconception about Pit Bulls is that their jaws lock when they bite. While it is true that the dogs have strong bites, their jaws work just the same way as any other dog's. Their jaws are strong because they are strong, in general. But, as long as a dog has no reason to bite, this is not an issue. The Pit Bull's bite should only be a concern when you're deciding on types of chew toys to get. This breed is not more likely to bite than any other dog. In fact, they are probably less likely to bite a human than some other breeds. Even when bred to fight bulls, these dogs were bred specifically not to bite humans.

It's also a myth that these dogs have a natural urge to fight and are dangerous. Dogs are only aggressive because they're reacting to something that's causing them a great amount of fear or stress. A properly bred Pit Bull has calm and gentle parents. Plus, if you put any dog into a bad situation, like being forced into a ring with another scared dog, it's only normal for them to protect themselves. A dog in a safe, healthy environment with a good temperament has no reason to be aggressive. Remember, a dog is only bad because humans have caused it to be bad. A properly bred and well-cared-for dog should not have dangerous or aggressive tendencies.

# Is a Pit Bull Right for Me?

Some breeds are best suited for particular owners. Before bringing a new dog home, it's important to take an honest look at your personality and capabilities. While you might mesh well with one breed, you might face challenges with another. Therefore, it's important to understand what a Pit Bull requires before bringing one into your home.

First of all, you must make sure that your town allows Pit Bull breeds. You don't want to suffer the trauma of getting your little one adjusted into their new home, only to have your dog taken away from you. If your town does not allow these breeds, by all means, advocate for these dogs. However, think carefully about breaking laws to keep a Pit Bull as a pet.

*Photo Courtesy of Bryan Olsen-Santana*

Also, consider how much time you have to devote to a dog. Pit Bulls cling tightly to their owners and need lots of positivity and attention. If you work a lot and don't have a lot of time to devote to your Pit Bull, this might not be the right dog for you. You don't want your dog to suffer separation anxiety because you don't have the time or energy to play with your dog.

This commitment also applies to exercise. If you're not an outdoorsy person and you hate going on walks, the Pit Bull might not be for you. Pit Bulls are high energy dogs that need an owner who can ensure they get the exercise they need. On a daily basis, this dog will need to go on a few walks and have plenty of play time. This dog cannot be a couch potato, so an owner who is motivated to exercise with the Pit Bull is necessary.

While this dog is fine with a lot of people in the home, it might not do as well if your house is full of pets. Every dog is different, but the Pit Bull may not get along very well with other animals. You don't want to worry about your Pit Bull chasing your cats around the house while you're gone, nor do you want to fear that your Pit Bull is uncomfortable with other dogs. While it's absolutely possible to have a Pit Bull share a space with another animal, this breed might be best as an only dog.

If your home fits the description of the ideal home for a Pit Bull, then it's time to start looking for the perfect dog for you! If not, you may want to reconsider if the Pit Bull is the right breed for you. Or, you may want to reevaluate your household and your habits so you can be ready for a Pit Bull when the time is right.

Despite their bad reputation, Pit Bulls are fantastic family pets. They are sweet, friendly, and playful. They get along great with kids and love to have fun. They are smart and able to learn cool skills. If your home is ready for a new dog, a Pit Bull is a fantastic choice for your new best friend.

## CHAPTER 2
# Choosing a Pit Bull

*"Pitbulls are really loving and intelligent, when bred and raised the right way for the first 8 weeks; there is no other dog that can compare to them."*

***Edward Genther***
*Blue Passion Kennel*

When you're ready to find the perfect dog, there are some things you'll want to take into account. First, you'll want to decide if you want to buy your Pit Bull from a breeder or if you want to adopt. If you choose to buy, you'll need to find a reputable breeder to make sure you have a healthy and ethically bred dog. If you want to adopt, you'll want to make sure you can fulfill all of the necessary requirements. Finally, you'll need to pick out the right Pit Bull for you. It's a lot more work than just picking out a cute puppy from a store, but all of the research will be worth it when you have your perfect pup in your home.

# Buying vs. Adopting

There is no right or wrong answer when it comes to deciding what is best for you and your household. There are a lot of pros and cons to take into consideration when deciding whether to buy or adopt. Don't let other people try to influence this decision based on their bias. In the end, you know what you want in a dog.

Photo Courtesy of Lindsey Hauser

There are some benefits when it comes to buying a dog from a breeder. If you have a good breeder, you know that you'll end up with a good dog. In many cases, friendliness and gentle temperaments are bred into a dog. If the pup's parents and their parents have desirable behavioral traits, it's likely that you'll see those same good traits in the pup. Also, if there's a specific breed or mix you're after, a breeder can give you a pretty good idea of how their pups are going to turn out. So, if you have your heart set on a Pit Bull with a specific look, you can find the right breeder for that mix. With a good breeder, you'll know that your dog is healthy and probably won't suffer from many genetic diseases later on in life. That will give you some peace of mind that with proper care, your little buddy will be around for many years to come.

On the other hand, buying a well-bred dog is not cheap. Prepare to spend anywhere from five hundred to fifteen hundred dollars on a good dog. This money comes from the breeder's expertise, their stock, and all of the time and care they put into taking care of pups. However, if you're after a certain kind of pup, the money may be well worth it.

Adoption is another great way to find your perfect Pit Bull. There are so many Pit Bull breeds in shelters that need good homes. There's a misconception that dogs in shelters are not good dogs because someone gave them up. This is not the case and there are many reasons why good dogs are surrendered. In some cases, there might be conflicts between the dog and owner, but this does not mean that there isn't a better home for this dog. For example, the owner may have had problems with the Pit Bull because the home already had another dog. The Pit Bull may have shown signs of stress that were interpreted as aggression. In a home with only people, this dog could be as gentle as can be.

*Photo Courtesy of*
*Lindsey Luimes*

Instead of finding a problem dog, you may end up finding a shelter dog that is good and pure. Because these dogs have an incorrect reputation for being brutes, many people buy them with the thought that the dog will be a good watchdog. When the new owner finds out that their Pit Bull isn't scaring anyone away, they might surrender the dog because they didn't expect it to be so soft. For someone who wants a sweetheart of a dog, adoption can be a great option.

Also, when you adopt a dog, you're giving a good home to a dog in need. Because you're not buying, you're lessening the demand for puppies, which keeps breeders from overproducing these breeds and overpopulating. By adopting, you're saving a life and helping responsible breeding practices.

On the other hand, you never know exactly what you're going to get when you adopt a dog. Perhaps you had your heart set on getting a puppy and there are only adults in the shelter. Or, the dogs in the shelter are good boys and girls, but something happened in their past life that makes them nervous around certain types of people or animals. It's better to find the right dog for your household, than to take the first one you find and hope for the best. If you know you need a certain type of Pit Bull in order to make the relationship work, perhaps it's best to buy from a breeder.

## How to Find a Reputable Breeder

Once you've decided that you're going to buy a puppy, it's time to look for a breeder. There are several reasons why you don't want to buy just any puppy. Especially when it comes to Pit Bulls, you want a breeder who cares about the safety and well-being of the dog. Good breeders are breed enthusiasts, not people trying to make a quick buck.

For example, you don't want to buy from someone who uses his or her dog for the intimidation factor. Bad breeders will purposefully breed aggression into dogs. Bad breeders also don't have the knowledge or care to make sure genetic diseases are bred out of the lineage. If you get the feeling that a breeder is not conducting good business practices and doesn't have the dogs' best interest in mind, avoid them. You don't want your

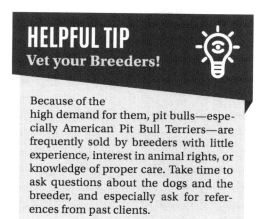

**HELPFUL TIP**
**Vet your Breeders!**

Because of the high demand for them, pit bulls—especially American Pit Bull Terriers—are frequently sold by breeders with little experience, interest in animal rights, or knowledge of proper care. Take time to ask questions about the dogs and the breeder, and especially ask for references from past clients.

hard-earned money to support someone who isn't helping the continuation of the breed.

An ethical breeder knows a lot about Pit Bull breeds and wants to help craft a better reputation for the dogs. They understand that Pit Bulls should be sweet, friendly family dogs. This breeder should be vetting their potential clients as much as their clients are vetting them. This will ensure that every pup is going to a good home.

Once you narrow down your search, get in touch with the breeders. If possible, visit their home and kennel. Meet the dogs so you get a good idea about what your puppy will be like. Make sure that all facilities are comfortable and clean for the dogs. During this time, ask questions about the breed. The breeder is an expert on this breed, so they should be enthusiastic about answering your questions. They might even ask you a few questions to make sure their dogs are a good fit for you. You want to feel comfortable with your breeder because they're going to be a valuable resource as you raise your dog. They should be willing to stay in contact with you, even after they cash your check.

## Health Tests, Certifications, and Breeder Guarantees

When visiting with your breeder, ask them if they provide any health tests or certifications. Typically, this comes in the form of a certificate from the vet, stating that the dogs they use for breeding are in good health. If the parents are in good health, that generally means that the pups will be healthy, too.

Some breeders will even suggest that the new owners take the pups to the vet within a few weeks, just to double-check that the puppies are healthy. This gives both you and the breeder peace of mind that your pup is in good shape. This way, the breeder is not liable if your dog is sick or injured later in life, and you know that your breeder had bred a good dog.

19

## Choosing Your Pup

Once you've picked out a breeder, it's time to choose a pup. Many people will just pick the cutest dog out of the bunch. While this is a perfectly valid way to choose a pup, you might also want to consider the dog's personality. Even well-bred litters will have some variation between pups, just like all siblings in a human family are a little bit different.

If you have the option to pick your pup from the litter, in person, give yourself a little time to hang out with all of the puppies and get to know their unique personalities. While you're playing with the pups, you're looking for one that falls in the middle range of all the personalities. You don't want the most dominant and rambunctious one, nor do you want the pup that's so shy it can't approach you. You definitely want to have a connection with the pup. Choose the one that's curious, but can be alone, too. These dogs usually have good temperaments as adults. The way you raise your Pit Bull will have a lot to do with how they turn out as adults, but genetics does play a role here.

## Pit Bull Rescues

Because of all the troubles with the Pit Bull breed, there are many organizations that rescue Pit Bulls and adopt them out to good homes. These organizations are very passionate about caring for a breed that often has a hard time finding a good home. Many of their rescues come from fighting rings or other abusive situations.

Because these organizations are so protective of their rescues, you have to be able to pass a test of sorts to adopt one of these Pit Bulls. If you read the first chapter and you thought a Pit Bull was the right fit for you, then you're well on your way! Before adoption, the rescue will want to know about everyone who lives at your home. They will also want to know about your past experiences with pets. Your home type and backyard situation will also factor into their decision to let you adopt.

Finally, they might even come to your home for an inspection, and do a follow-up visit later on. It may seem extreme, but it's in the dog's and owner's best interests.

If you're still trying to figure out if a Pit Bull is right for you, you may want to consider fostering a dog. This allows you to act as the owner for a short period of time until someone is able to adopt the dog. You'll keep the dog in your home and work on socialization skills. And, if you decide that you want to keep the dog, you can always adopt! Keep in mind that you'll have to undergo the vetting process to be able to foster a dog.

# Tips for Adopting a Pit Bull

Photo Courtesy of Deineira Smith

You may be tempted to rescue the first Pit Bull you see at the pound, but you should still make sure that the dog is right for you. A rescue may be shy at first, so give the dog a little time to warm up to you. However, this breed is supposed to be friendly, so one that's painfully shy may cause you some issues later on.

Make sure to take the dog out on a trial run. You want the dog to meet all of its potential new family members and any other pets you keep in your home. If problems arise, you may need to reconsider the dog or make adjustments to your home. The shelter may not have a lot of information on the dog's back story, but hopefully they can tell you if they have noticed anything important about the dog, like if he gets along fine with cats or if he is frightened by large men. Some quirks can be trained out, but other issues may be difficult to work through. Don't rush into a decision—take your time to make sure everyone in the situation will be happy.

It's easy to rush into buying or adopting a dog the moment you decide you want a Pit Bull, but if you're patient, you'll find the right dog. When choosing whether to adopt or buy from a breeder, take your household and personal interests into account. If you're buying, make sure to only give business to breeders who are knowledgeable about the breed and care about their pups. When you take the time to choose the right dog, you're making a great first step in your dog's new life at your home.

# CHAPTER 3
# Preparing Your Household for Your Pit Bull

You may know exactly where you're going to get your new Pit Bull, but before you bring your pup home, it's important to prepare for your new friend. Because pups can't be taken away from their mother until they're a few months old, this gives you plenty of time to get everything ready for your new dog. Bringing a new dog into your established home and routine can be stressful, and this stress can affect how you get along with your new dog. So, to help everyone involved feel at ease, take the time to get your household ready for your new pup.

## Getting Children and Pets Ready

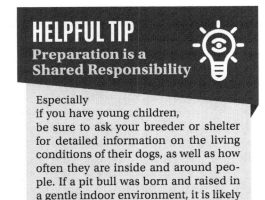

**HELPFUL TIP**
**Preparation is a Shared Responsibility**

Especially if you have young children, be sure to ask your breeder or shelter for detailed information on the living conditions of their dogs, as well as how often they are inside and around people. If a pit bull was born and raised in a gentle indoor environment, it is likely to adjust just fine to your home.

Chances are, your new Pit Bull will take to children very quickly. However, it's still important to make sure everyone feels comfortable. It's not uncommon for unfortunate incidents to happen because a child has overwhelmed a dog. Pit Bulls are naturally patient around children, but accidents can happen with any breed. For this reason, it's important to teach children how to act around dogs.

Children will likely become very excited at the sight of a cute puppy. Young children are curious and will want to poke and prod the dog. They might not know that their actions can be painful or scary to a dog that doesn't know what's going on. A dog's natural reaction is to give off signals that they're stressed or scared. As a very last resort, they may snap or bite. Of course, this generally takes place when children are too rough. A Pit Bull doesn't snap without reason.

Teach your children how to properly pet a dog. For little kids, gently petting the dog's back is safest. Tell your child that the head (including the eyes, ears, nose, and mouth) is off limits, and the tail should not be pulled. Also, tell them to use soft voices around the dog. These are all things that can make a dog feel more comfortable. You can also teach your kids how your dog communicates. A tail between the legs, bared teeth, and growling are all signs that your dog needs some space.

With any breed, adult supervision is necessary when kids and dogs mix. You can lecture kids about proper behavior around dogs, but it won't always prevent a pup from getting poked in the eye. Monitor kids and correct their behavior while monitoring your dog's behavior. With any luck, your kids

Photo Courtesy of Jaco &Judith Swanepoel

will soon learn how to respect animals and your dog will feel comfortable in your home.

It's trickier to prepare your pets for a new arrival. It's hard for your furry children to understand why there's suddenly a new dog running around the house. The process of getting your pets acclimated to your new Pit Bull is especially important because this breed doesn't always take to other pets very well. You can't just bring a Pit Bull home and hope for the best. Before you can even commit to a new Pit Bull, you must make sure he gets along with the other animals.

First, set up a meeting on neutral territory. This will prevent your existing pets from getting territorial. A friend's backyard or a park works well. Don't force the animals together, but allow them to sniff each other on their own time. It helps to have both animals on leashes, so a friend's assistance is necessary. If the dogs get along, allow them to continue to check each other out. If there is conflict, calmly separate the animals. If there are issues, it doesn't necessarily mean that the dogs will never get along. You can always try reintroducing them once everyone has had time to settle down.

Next, reintroduce the pets in your home. This will give you a better idea of how they will act in a familiar space. Again, keep the pets on a leash until they prove they can handle going off-leash. A few different meetings are necessary to make sure the pets will get along in different situations. Finally, let the dogs off the leash and allow them to play. If they get along well, then there's a good chance the new Pit Bull will work out. Even if the animals get along, you will need to continue supervising them for quite some time. Dogs can be unpredictable and exhibit strange behaviors when you least expect it.

# Household Dangers

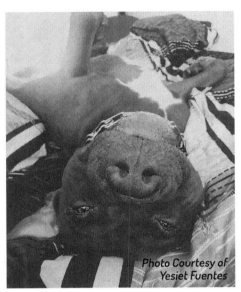

Photo Courtesy of
Yesiet Fuentes

If you were to bring a new baby home, you would spend plenty of time baby-proofing your home to protect the infant from all of the kid-unfriendly things a home can hold. A new puppy is no different. You'll need to think like a dog and pick up everything that can cause a little pup harm. Here are a few things to keep in mind while you're in the dog-proofing process.

Pit Bulls are notorious chewers, so anything you want to keep intact needs to be placed out of reach. In a dogless home, you may keep your shoes by the door. A puppy will monopolize on that the second you turn your back. Small objects will become choking hazards and exposed cords can cause electric shocks. If there's something you don't want your pup to put in their mouth, make sure it's completely out of reach.

You'd be surprised at how sneaky a determined Pit Bull can be. When a Pit Bull decides they're going to do something, little will get in their way. They will climb furniture and make daring leaps to get what they want. In some cases, items are not necessarily safe because they're on a table or in a cupboard. Crafty dogs have been known to open cupboards under the sink and get into cleaning chemicals. If this describes your dog, you may want to invest in some child locks.

If you're planning on letting your dog roam the backyard unattended, you'll need to do a quick check of the yard. Sticks can be fun for dogs to chew on, but a Pit Bull can easily snap one into tiny pieces, which can get lodged in the digestive tract. A curious dog might also get into forbidden treats like fertilizers and pesticides, which can make a dog very sick. Even plants can make your pup ill. If you have a lot of landscaping in your yard, you may want to research specific plants to see if they are toxic to dogs. Common plants like hastas, different types of ivy, and varieties of lilies can make a dog sick if they eat too much.

# Preparing Inside Spaces

Once the dangers are out of reach, you'll want to make your dog feel comfortable in your home. A dog should have a place of their own to go to when they're feeling stressed out. This is a spot that is off limits to humans. A dog bed or a crate works best, as it's a cozy spot for a pup.

If you're bringing home a new puppy, you'll want some way to contain them. As you'll find when it's time for potty training, it's best if the puppy isn't allowed to roam freely around the house. A temporary pen in your kitchen is helpful when your dog is small. It's not meant to be doggy prison, but a way to keep tabs on your dog when you're out and about. Or, a baby gate works wonders for keeping your dog contained within a room or two. Make sure to have plenty of chew toys around so your dog won't turn to your furniture to gnaw on. Also, fresh water should always be available for your dog to lap up at all hours of the day.

*Photo Courtesy of
Katie Yedinak*

# Preparing Outside Spaces

*"Pitbulls are escape artists, so you need to make sure your yard or the dog is secured to a tether when not supervised. Just because your dog is friendly in their environment does not mean they will be that way if they get lose."*

**James Jackson**
*Flatline Kennels*

Photo Courtesy of
Matt Faupel

If you plan on letting your dog spend time outside in the yard, you'll want to make sure everything is safe for him. A fence is a must. Not only does it keep your dog safe from running away, but it keeps your dog safe from people or animals that may intrude. Your dog will probably be as friendly as can be, but the mailperson may not see things the same way when your beefy Pit Bull comes bounding toward them during a delivery. For your dog's safety, a fence without any gaps to slip through is vital. In a pinch, a chain can give your dog some outside time without direct supervision, but it's not a long-term solution. This breed gets lonely easily and may feel neglected if they feel stuck in one spot outside. With a fence, your dog has a little room to run around and explore.

If you plan on letting your dog spend time in the yard unsupervised during the day, consider creating some kind of shelter for your dog. A doghouse or a spot with a blanket and some rain cover will keep your dog comfortable for a few hours. Pit Bulls have very short fur, so they get cold easily. But, because they have bulky bodies, they can also get overheated and sunburned if it's too hot outside. If you can't be outside for a few hours without some sort of protection, neither should your Pit Bull.

# Special Considerations to Make

While you're working on preparing your home for your Pit Bull, you may want to brush up on your city's ordinances regarding Pit Bull breeds. If your town has discriminatory laws, consider joining a group to advocate for these dogs. Or, if your dog park requires special muzzles or harnesses, think about tracking down these items before you bring your dog home. Or, you may decide to search for spaces where your dog is welcome. Also, if you live in an apartment complex or rent a home, double-check with your landlord to ensure that Pit Bull breeds are allowed. It would be unfair for the dog to start settling into a home, only to be removed shortly after. It's best to make accommodations and do research early on, so you don't have to worry about major adjustments when things don't go as expected.

Once your house is in order, you'll feel a lot better about bringing a new Pit Bull into the mix. Remember that this breed with put anything they find into their mouth, so it's best to keep your belongings completely out of reach. This applies to outdoor spaces, too. Give your dog a comfy place to chill out so he feels like a member of the family. At the same time, guard the rest of your home from the mess that is a new puppy. With a little preparation, your home will be ready for a new Pit Bull in no time!

Photo Courtesy of
Gianna Giordano

# CHAPTER 4
# Bringing Your Pit Bull Home

Finally, it's time to bring your new Pit Bull home! Hopefully, you've had plenty of time to prepare for your new friend. Even if your home is ready, there are still a few things you'll want to do to prepare for your dog. Some of these things can be done in the first week to give you some peace of mind that you won't be in a rush if a mishap occurs. Other tips will reduce stress in both you and your dog. A new dog can be a big life change, but with a little prep work, everything should go smoothly!

## Planning for Your Pit Bull

Photo Courtesy of
Jaco & Judith Swanepoel

While spontaneity is fun, there are a few reasons why you'll want to plan ahead before bringing your new dog home. One reason is because it's a ton of work taking care of a new dog, and it's difficult to watch your new puppy while you're trying to clean up the house and buy supplies. If you do some of the work before your dog comes home, you'll have more time to spend with your dog.

Another reason is because dogs can sense stress. Pit Bulls are sensitive dogs, which means that they pick up on human emotions and non-verbal cues. So, if you're stressed out and frantic about getting everything ready for your dog, your Pit Bull will know something is up and feel uncomfortable. On the other hand, if you're cool and relaxed, then your dog will have a reason to relax during a time that's a big transition. Your dog will already be a little nervous about going to a new home, so you'll want to do every little thing you can to make him feel more at ease.

# The First Night at Home

The first night at a new home can be a big change for a dog. Up until now, your Pit Bull has only known one home, which was shared with his mother and siblings. Now, he'll be transported to a new place in a strange car and will be surrounded by strange people. From a dog's perspective, this is a very scary time. However, there are a few things you can do to make things easier on your dog.

Make sure you have plenty of treats on hand. Treats are one of the best ways to show your dog that they're doing exactly what they're supposed to do. If they approach you, give them a treat. If they potty outside or lie on their bed, give them a treat. This is a small thing you can do to make your dog feel happy to be in your home. Exercise and play can also wear your dog out to the point where they won't feel as anxious as if they're just lying around. Plus, they'll have so much fun that they'll forget that they were ever worried about their new home in the first place!

Pit Bulls are companion dogs, so they're more likely to suffer from separation anxiety than other breeds. It's possible that your new dog will cry or become anxious at night because he wants to be close to you. However, not all owners want their dog to sleep on their bed. If you're planning on crate training, you may consider moving the crate near your bedroom so your dog doesn't feel so abandoned. Even if your dog isn't inside your room, setting the crate in the hallway with the door cracked open will let your dog know that you're near. As time goes on, you can move the crate out to wherever you prefer your dog to sleep.

Before bed, make sure your dog gets to go outside to use the bathroom. If you do this immediately before bed, your dog will be less likely to cry an hour later. However, you'll want to remember that puppies need to go outside very frequently, so you'll want your dog to be close enough that you can hear when they whine to go out.

# Going to the Vet

Even if you don't go to the vet in the first few weeks, you'll want to have a vet's contact information on hand. Puppies are notorious for swallowing things they find on the floor, so in the event of an emergency, it's good to have both a regular vet and an emergency vet in your phone book.

If you don't already have a vet, there are a few things to keep in mind when choosing one. Most people will just choose the vet closest to where they live, but there are more considerations one must make. Some vet clinics are small and do not have the full range of services. If your local clinic does not have a lab or surgery services, then you have to decide which services are important to you in a regular vet.

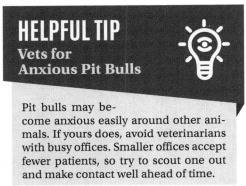

**HELPFUL TIP**

**Vets for Anxious Pit Bulls**

Pit bulls may become anxious easily around other animals. If yours does, avoid veterinarians with busy offices. Smaller offices accept fewer patients, so try to scout one out and make contact well ahead of time.

Also, it doesn't hurt to take recommendations from people who know local vets. Breeders are a great source because they already have an established relationship with a vet. Shelters and rescues can also suggest a vet because they probably work with the same vets on a regular basis. Or, just ask a friend who their trusted veterinarian is. You want this person to be someone you can trust because your dog's health is in their hands. Choose someone you feel comfortable asking questions and chatting with.

When you do take your dog to the vet for the first time, make sure to make it a positive experience. Many dogs get nervous at the vet because something has happened in the past that they didn't like. Before you go, make sure your dog has had plenty of exercise so their playful energy doesn't turn into anxious energy. From the moment you get into the car, start praising your dog for staying calm and give lots of treats. If your dog walks by your side into the building, give them another treat. During the checkup, the vet will probably give your dog treats, too.

To prepare your dog for the vet, practice touching your dog as a vet might. Pretend to look in his ears, pull back his lips to see his teeth, and gently palpate his belly. Some uncomfortable experiences, like having his temperature taken and getting shots, are best left to the professionals. But if your dog is comfortable being touched in this manner and being petted by other people, then your dog shouldn't have a problem at the vet. Again, this is a situation where you want to act like everything is fine so your dog doesn't get any ideas to the contrary.

# Puppy Classes

Photo Courtesy of Brendan Sloan

Within the first few months of having your dog home, you should consider enrolling in a puppy training course. Not only will this give your dog the skills they need to start their training, but it will help them socialize with other dogs. As we will discuss in a later chapter, socialization is an important part of a dog's life that ideally takes place when the pup is between four and eight months old. When you let your dog interact with other dogs, he will be more likely to get along with others as an adult, provided these interactions go well.

These classes are also just as valuable to the owner as they are to a dog. If you've never trained a dog before, this is a good introduction to dog training. An experienced trainer will teach you how to give commands and reward your dog for successfully completing the command. Your weekly class is a time where you can ask an expert questions about your dog's behavior and get answers based off of experience. Also, you'll have someone you can contact when you have questions after the class is finished. It's nice to have lots of resources for when you need help with your dog. As an added bonus, these puppy classes will teach your dog basic skills that will make them a little more manageable as their puppy energy comes in full force.

# Pet Supplies to Have Ready

It's hard to know exactly what you need when getting a new dog, but there are lots of things you'll want to have on hand before you even bring your dog home. For starters, you'll want a crate (if you're planning on crate training) or a bed. Sturdy food and water dishes that cannot easily be destroyed are also necessary. When it comes to a collar and leash, you'll probably want to start off with a flat, buckled collar. There are different kinds of leashes on the market, but a sturdy, nylon leash works best. You don't want anything too long or too short, so stick with the 4-foot or 6-foot varieties. You may be tempted to get a retractable leash, but this may reinforce bad walking habits. Besides, Pit Bulls are strong, determined dogs. If your dog sprints after a squirrel on a walk, a retractable leash may snap.

*Photo Courtesy of Meredith Duncan*

Next, you'll need plenty of toys. Pit Bulls love sturdy chew toys and tug ropes. Stay away from stuffed animals that can be ripped to shreds because they can become a choking hazard. There are lots of toys made especially for strong chewers, so pick something you know will last. Puzzle toys, like Kong toys, can be a lot of fun for a dog and will keep them busy. Stock up on these toys because they will wear out quickly.

You'll also want some grooming supplies. A natural (or synthetic) bristled brush is enough to keep shedding fur from covering your house and will give your dog a nice shine. Nail clippers will keep their claws from scratching you when they hop up on the couch to cuddle. A gentle shampoo is also good to have on hand when your Pit Bull inevitably rolls in the mud (or worse) and gets dirty. You'll also want a toothbrush and toothpaste that's made for dogs to keep your dog's teeth healthy and fresh.

Finally, you'll need a good-quality dog food and plenty of tasty treats. Choosing a dog food will be covered in a later chapter. It's good to have a couple types of treats on hand so your dog will always be motivated to behave well. A high-value treat is a powerful tool.

# How Much Will This Cost?

It's hard to predict just how much a new dog will cost you. There are so many factors to consider and so many ways to either spend a lot, or a little, when it comes to each factor. For example, if you're buying a Pit Bull from a good breeder, it will cost anywhere between $500 and $1,500. Shelters and rescues usually charge a fee because their dogs are up to date on their shots and are spayed or neutered. Even then, you can adopt a dog for a hundred dollars, on average.

Up front, you'll feel like you're spending a lot of money on supplies. But many of these supplies will be used for many years. Dishes, crates, and leashes will last for a long time, so you'll only have to purchase them once or twice throughout your dog's life. If you add up everything in the previous section, it will cost you around $200–$400. Food can cost an additional $600 or so a year.

At least once a year, you'll need to take your dog to the vet for a checkup and shots. These routine visits can cost between $100 and $200. You'll also need flea and tick preventative and heartworm medicine, which costs several hundred dollars a year.

When you add all of this up, it's possible that you'll spend over a thousand dollars just in the first year of your dog's life. This seems like a lot, but it's well worth it. After all, your new Pit Bull will be a part of the family in no time!

It takes a lot of work just to get ready for a new dog, but if you've made it this far, you're ready to start raising your new Pit Bull pup. During the first few months, you may feel like you're shelling out a ton of money on vet visits, supplies, and classes, but it will get easier as time goes on.

Photo Courtesy of Samantha Fey

# CHAPTER 5
# Puppy Parenting

If you've never owned a puppy before, you will be amazed at how much work it can be! One can not simply bring a puppy home and expect to let them roam free and behave like a good houseguest. Without proper training and boundaries, puppies will act like wild animals because that's just their natural instinct. Of course, one cannot truly compare raising a puppy to raising a child, but there are definitely some similarities. A dog owner must prepare their puppy for adulthood so they grow up to be a good doggy citizen and family member. This type of training starts the moment you bring your dog home. This process can be a struggle but it's worth the hard work when your dog grows out of the puppy stage and into an awesome adult.

# Standing By Your Expectations

Perhaps you already have an idea of how you want your dog to act in your home. This varies from owner to owner. Some are satisfied if their dog doesn't completely destroy the house and are more lenient with other pesky behaviors. Some owners plan to be stricter and want their pooch to stay off of furniture and stay silent in the house. There is no sin-

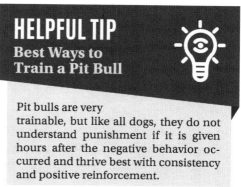

**HELPFUL TIP**

**Best Ways to Train a Pit Bull**

Pit bulls are very trainable, but like all dogs, they do not understand punishment if it is given hours after the negative behavior occurred and thrive best with consistency and positive reinforcement.

gle way to raise a dog and you can make as many or as few rules as you like. However, once you decide upon a few rules, it's important to stick to them.

For instance, you may have nice new couches in your house. Pit Bulls will shed tiny hairs on any surface where they spend a lot of time, not to mention their dirty paws after a game of fetch. It's perfectly reasonable to demand that your dog stays on the floor. However, to properly enforce this kind of behavior, it's important to keep this rule. If you've given your Pit Bull a bath and they're clean enough to be on your couch, it's not a good idea to let them hop up for one special occasion.

One reason behind this is that dogs have a hard time understanding conditions. They will not recognize that they're dirty and that you don't want dirt on your couch. They'll just see a comfy spot to cuddle with their owner. It's easier to teach a dog that the couch is forbidden, but their dog bed is a nice place to rest, than to scold them for jumping on the couch when they're not freshly bathed.

Of course, you may change your expectations once you bring your dog home. Sometimes there are fights you don't care to put up. Perhaps you decided that your bed is going to be a pet-free zone, but you really like to snuggle with your Pit Bull before bed. As long as you revise your expectations and create some consistency, it's perfectly normal to change your mind about how you expect your dog to behave.

Photo Courtesy of
Aalihya Waizenegger
James Bohm with Brandi

# Crate Training

When bringing a new dog home, crate training is something you'll want to seriously consider. There are lots of benefits to crate training and it's much easier to teach when your dog is a puppy as opposed to an adult. When used correctly, a crate is a cozy spot for your dog to hang out in when he feels overwhelmed or stressed out. It's also a good way to keep your puppy under control for short periods of time when you cannot watch them, like if you have to run to the store and your dog has yet to take control of their bladder. It's also a great way to keep your dog safe while traveling in a car. A crate is

Photo Courtesy of Kade Peterson

not a "doggy prison" to lock your Pit Bull in when they're being naughty, nor is it ideal to lock your dog up for an entire workday. There are other solutions to those problems that are much better for your dog.

Starting out, your pup might be a little wary of spending time in a dark box. It's better to slowly ease them into the crate instead of stuffing them in there and shutting the front. Put a comfy blanket inside and scatter a few toys or bones in there. At first, you might drop a treat by the entrance and stand back, letting your pup explore on their own time. If they feel comfortable, they'll go for the treat. Once your dog takes the first treat, place treats further back in the crate until they're willing to go to the very back for it.

Next, place food and water dishes in the crate. If your dog is comfortable with exploring the crate, they'll be willing to hop in and eat their meals in the crate. The prospect of eating will be very enticing to a puppy and will cause them to like the crate because it gives them yummy food. After a few meals, try closing the front of the crate while they eat. Hopefully, they'll be too busy eating to notice that you've done anything.

Once your dog feels safe being enclosed in the crate, build up time spent inside the crate. Start with a minute or two and reward your dog for staying calm. Eventually, you'll want your pup to be able to take naps inside for at least an hour without becoming distressed. As long as you make all crate experiences positive, your pup is unlikely to resist spending time inside their cozy nook.

37

# Chewing

All puppies, but especially Pit Bulls, are big chewers. Part of this is because they're growing adult teeth and chewing helps the new teeth poke through. Another reason is because dogs chew for entertainment and to reduce stress. Your Pit Bull will chew on objects no matter what, so it's good to give them direction about what they should chew on and what they should avoid.

One way to encourage productive chewing is by having chew toys readily available. Once your dog gets the urge to gnaw on something, they won't change their mind because they didn't find a bone. Instead, they will choose to chew on your shoes, the remote, a chair, or whatever else is handy You'll also want to praise them when they take a toy to chew on and firmly tell them "no" when you catch them chewing on a forbidden item, before redirecting them to an acceptable chew.

Purchase sturdy items for your Pit Bull. Ropes, rawhides, deer antlers, and sturdy bones are a good place to start. You want to avoid anything too small that might cause your dog to choke, or anything that can easily fall apart or splinter. Once your puppy outgrows chews designed for little mouths, upgrade to something bigger and sturdier.

If you find that your dog chews on your belongings, there are a few things you can do to avoid this in the future. One way to deal with this is to always keep an eye on your dog and correct them whenever they put their mouth around something forbidden. Unfortunately, this is hard to do, so you'll also want to avoid leaving your belongings where your dog can get to them. Finally, if your dog resorts to gnawing on table legs and other furniture, there are deterrent sprays that are safe for dogs but make your furniture taste terrible to them. This strategy might be useful as a last resort.

# Barking

Most dogs will bark for any number of reasons. Maybe your dog sees another dog across the street. Or, there could be someone at your door and your dog's trying to notify you. Or, maybe your dog is barking at you because he wants to play. Regardless of the reason, excessive barking can be very annoying to you and people in your area.

If your dog's barking is driving you nuts, try to correct the behavior. When they bark, give them a firm "no." When they're quiet, praise them by saying something like, "good no bark!" You may also find that their barking is set off by particular stimuli. For instance, if your dog barks whenever someone is at the door, you may try to avoid this behavior by telling your dog to lie down on their bed whenever the doorbell rings. That way, it forces them to do a job, hopefully distracting them from their barking.

# Digging

You may find that your pup is interested in creating holes in the backyard when he's left alone to sniff around. This becomes a problem if he digs too far and makes a burrow under the fence or digs up all of your plants. This is another puppy behavior that requires constant vigilance to stop. If your dog is a digger, you'll need to catch them in the act so you can correct them. When you see them digging, clap loudly to catch their attention. Some people like to use a can filled with rocks because the sound is more attention-grabbing. Once your dog breaks their focus, give them a firm "no." Once they stop, try to distract them from the digging by throwing a ball or something else that will break their focus and put their mind someplace else.

Another way to deter your dog from being naughty when they're outside is by using outside time for activities only until they can be trusted to behave well on their own. Tire your Pit Bull out with a game of fetch or something that gets their heart rate going. They'll be so tired from playing that they won't have the energy to be destructive.

# Biting

Puppies use their mouths to make sense of the world around them, just like people use their hands to discover new things. Over time, a dog will learn how hard they can bite down when playing with other dogs but as a puppy, this is a skill they're still working to master. When puppies play together, they will inevitably chomp down too hard on a sibling. When this happens, the other puppy will yelp, teaching the first puppy that they must be more gentle.

Even though Pit Bulls are notoriously gentle, they might still try out their bite response with people. This is not an aggressive response, but just the way your puppy makes sense of what humans are like. This is generally not painful, but can be a little uncomfortable. It's also something you don't want your dog to make a habit of.

To break your puppy of their nibbling ways, speak to them in dog language. If they nibble on you, make a high-pitched yelp like a fellow puppy. This will probably startle them because they understand that a yelp means they're playing too rough. Continue to do this until you break them of their nibbling. While your puppy is in the biting stage, pay special attention to who your dog interacts with. Instruct your houseguests to take part in this training by yelping if the dog bites, reminding them that your dog is not dangerous, but only learning.

# Separation Anxiety

Photo Courtesy of Francesca Visani

Pit Bulls are sensitive companion animals who always want to be by your side. This makes them great pets, but it also makes it hard when you have to leave them alone for any period of time. Some dogs will get so worked up at your absence that they will develop separation anxiety. A mild case will manifest in crying and whimpering when you leave. More serious cases will cause dogs to have accidents in the house and destroy all of your belongings. While some dogs experience a little separation anxiety, serious anxiety is not good for your dog and can cause health and behavioral issues.

One way to prevent separation anxiety is by watching your behavior around your dog in particularly stressful situations. When you leave the house, do you give your dog hugs and kisses and make a big production of your pending absence? When you return, do you greet your dog in a high-pitched voice? These are actions that tell your dog that your absence is a big deal and that they should take notice. Instead, calmly and quietly leave and return to your house like nothing is wrong. This should help your dog to relax because they know you're going to come and go without incident.

Another thing you can do to help anxiety is by keeping your dog too busy and tired to feel anxious. If your dog freaks out when you leave for work in the morning, maybe try increasing the amount of exercise they get early in the morning. That way, they will be more likely to sleep during the day. There are also fun puzzle toys that require your dog to work to get a treat out. These can be given to your dog as you leave, keeping them active in a time they might otherwise be panicking.

If nothing you try helps, you may want to talk to your vet about other solutions. A vet usually does not prescribe medication for long-term use, but may recommend natural supplements that can ease your dog's worry. Of course, before trying any of these supplements, talk to a vet to make sure your dog can handle it.

If you have a new puppy, you'll need someone to be around to let them out to use the bathroom on a very frequent basis. If you're unable to run home to do so, it might be beneficial to enroll your dog in a daycare or hire a dog walker. If they have that extra bit of attention during the day, they will be less likely to destroy your home because they had too much nervous energy and no way to deal with it.

# Bedtime

Dogs do not run on the same sleep schedule as humans. They are more likely to go hard for a few hours, then sleep when there's nothing exciting going on. It's totally normal for dogs to snooze half the day away. However, people have sleep schedules for good reasons, so your dog will need to learn how to run on their owner's schedule.

This can be done by setting a regular schedule. Over time, your dog will learn that they must be quiet and allow you to sleep. To do this, take your dog to use the bathroom the very last thing you do before bed. If you're using a crate, put your dog in the crate and go to bed. If your dog starts whimpering immediately, try to ignore it the best you can. Eventually, they will settle down and get some rest. You might find that they are crying just a few hours later. If this occurs, they probably have to use the bathroom. After you take your dog out, repeat the process of putting them in their kennel and going to bed. Try not to make a lot of noise, or they might think it's time to get up. When you take your dog out in the middle of the night, this is for business only. Playing with them or giving them lots of attention may make them think it's time to play again.

The puppy stage can be very difficult, especially to a first time owner, but it goes by so fast. When you find yourself getting frustrated with all of the work, remember that you will one day long for those puppy years. It can be easy to give up on training during this time, but it's important to keep working at it. The more you teach your dog in their early weeks and months, the easier it will be to continue training in their adult years. If you prevent bad habits from forming, you won't have to work as hard to break them of the habits later.

Photo Courtesy of
BrookLinn Clark

# CHAPTER 6
# **Housetraining**

Housetraining will likely test your limits with your new dog. You'll have to drop everything and go outside when your dog has the urge to go. You'll also have to clean up stinky messes when your dog doesn't make it outside. Some say that dogs can only hold it for as many hours as they are months old. So, a three-month-old puppy will likely only be able to hold it for about three hours. Your patience will be tested constantly for weeks on end. Don't give up! Eventually, your puppy will learn how to use the potty outside and you'll no longer have to clean up messes indoors. Stick with it, and before long, your dog will be housetrained.

*Photo Courtesy of Kourtney Earles*

# Different Options for Potty Training

Though the most ideal potty training method is taking your dog outside to potty, it's not the only way to prevent accidents. There are lots of different products in pet stores that offer alternatives if you're concerned that your dog is going to destroy your home with their accidents.

Photo Courtesy of Gage Hatfield

Lots of new puppy parents use newspaper in a crate or pen to easily dispose of messes. Pet stores sell puppy pads, which are absorbent pads that contain enzymes so dogs are attracted to the scent and choose to relieve themselves on the pads. Once the dog has used it, you can easily throw it away. If your dog is going to potty on the floor, some owners like to train their dogs to at least do it somewhere that is easy to clean up. Similar to these pads are litter box– like devices that mimic grass. If you live in an area where it's not easy to go outside when your dog has to go, you may choose to train your dog to use an indoor potty. These are made to be easy to clean and attractive to a puppy.

If you plan on using an indoor potty product until your dog is able to hold it for longer, be aware that your dog might not transition to using the bathroom outside when they grow up. Oftentimes, habits are instilled in dogs as puppies, so it's a little harder to break them of certain habits as they age. That's not to say that it's impossible to housetrain an adult dog, but it can be challenging. For this reason, if you have the ability to take your Pit Bull outside to use the facilities, then that's the best option. If not, know that there are other back-up options available for you to use.

# The First Few Weeks

Potty training is difficult because it requires constant attention. Your dog can only learn when they have a successful attempt and receive praise. Because of this, you will spend a lot of time outside, coaxing your dog to go potty, even if they only went thirty minutes ago. Aim to make a trip outside sooner than when you figure your dog will need to go. For example, if your dog urinates every two hours or so, try to take him out before that two-hour mark. If you find yourself getting distracted and forgetting, set a timer each time you come back inside. If you wait for the whining, it may be too late.

When you take your dog out, try to go to the same spot every time. When dogs use the bathroom, their urine produces scent markers that tell your dog that they've found their spot.  When they smell this, they are likely to potty there again. This will prevent you from traversing all over the neighborhood with a dog that doesn't know what you want out of them. If they smell their spot, they'll understand what they're supposed to do.

Photo Courtesy of
Jaco &Judith Swanepoel

# Rewarding Positive Behavior

The right reward system is vital when housetraining your dog. In order to teach your dog something new that goes against their instincts, you must think like a dog. Dogs learn best through positive reinforcement. Though it may be your parenting instinct to use punishment, this is not effective when it comes to housetraining a dog.

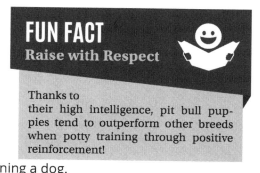

**FUN FACT**
**Raise with Respect**

Thanks to their high intelligence, pit bull puppies tend to outperform other breeds when potty training through positive reinforcement!

One common mistake that dog owners make is that they punish their dog for accidents. Unfortunately, this does nothing but cause dogs to be afraid of their owner. When some owners see an accident, they get angry at their dog. They might also rub their dog's nose in the accident to remind them of what they've done wrong. However, this does nothing to remind the dog of their prior accident. A dog is not able to recall past events in this way and will be confused as to why their owner is yelling at them. This kind of behavior will upset a sensitive dog like a Pit Bull. When a dog learns to be afraid in relation to having accidents, your dog will continue to have accidents, but will likely do a better job of hiding them.

Instead of catching your dog having accidents after the fact, you must either prevent the accident or catch them in the act. This takes a lot of attention on the owner's part. However, the payoff is that your dog learns how to go outside faster. Proactive measures are always better than reactive measures when it comes to training dogs. If you take your dog outside before they have to go, they can be rewarded with a treat and praise when they go potty. This positive result will make them more likely to repeat the behavior so they can get that reward. With a lot of practice, using the bathroom outside will become natural.

If you do catch your dog in the middle of having an accident, try to correct their behavior. After a while, you'll know when your dog is about ready to squat or lift their leg. When you see these cues, clap or make a noise to get your dog's attention. Then try to get them outside as quickly as possible. If your dog makes it outside, give them a treat and lots of praise. If they don't make it, clean it up and move on. You'll have another learning opportunity in an hour or so.

# Crate Training for Housetraining

Easier potty training is another benefit to crate training. The crate acts as a little wolf den, which dogs naturally want to keep clean. A dog is not willing to soil their immediate resting quarters unless there is no other option. If your dog is in an appropriately sized crate, they won't be cramped, but they also won't have space to soil their crate and still be comfortable. You may still choose to place an absorbent pad on the floor of the crate to make clean-up easier in case of an accident. This is a great way to cut down on accidents and to prevent messes when you're not around to watch your dog. However, it's important to never use the crate as punishment.

# Playpens and Doggy Doors

Photo Courtesy of
Megan Maden

If you don't plan on using a crate, there are other tools that can help you with your housetraining. Because puppies can cause chaos, it is sometimes useful to keep them contained. Again, a dog pen should never be used as puppy prison, but as a method of keeping track of your dog's actions while you're unable to keep a close eye on them. The pen should allow them plenty of room to play, but can also contain puppy pads, newspapers, or other mess-containing objects. You may also find that your dog does not want to soil their pen and will do their best to wait until you can take them outside.

If your dog is getting the hang of potty training and you trust them to go outside when they need to, you might consider installing a dog door. This can be useful if you need to be away from the home for a while and your dog can be trusted to come and go as they please. However, be advised that other things besides the dog can pass through the door. Your dog can carry indoor things outside and outside things inside.

# Hiring Help

If you work outside the home and are unable to let your puppy out every couple of hours, it might be best to hire some extra help to get you through the housetraining stage. Hiring dog walkers and dog sitters is as easy as clicking a few buttons on an app. You can work out the terms of the service with the dog walker and someone can stop by as often as you need to give your dog a little extra attention, or you can drop your dog off at the sitter's house on your way to work. Another option is to drop your little pup off at daycare. Doggy daycare centers often allow for half day or whole day services, plus weekends.

Photo Courtesy of BrookLinn Clark

Not only will someone ensure that your dog gets outside when they need to, but they will also make sure your dog is entertained and well cared for while you're at work. It can be expensive to hire extra help, especially if you need a lot of it, but your dog will slowly become more independent. In time, your dog can handle being alone for a work day, as long as you stop by over lunch to let your little buddy out to pee.

Before long, you'll forget that there was ever a period of time where your dog was having accidents in the house and begging to go out every hour. Until then, remember to stay patient. Your dog will learn the fastest through positive reinforcement. Anger and punishments will only set them back further. There are lots of tools and resources around you to assist you through this crucial teaching moment, so don't feel like you have to tackle housetraining without help.

# CHAPTER 7
# Socialization

*"Socialization must be started early. Our pups are socialized with 10 to 12 adult dogs starting at 4 weeks of age. If socialization is started to late that's where problems happen. Start socializing as early as possible."*

**Edward Genther**
*Blue Passion Kenne*

Many people don't realize that socialization is an extremely important part of a dog's life. Not all dogs are naturally good with other dogs or people. It takes the right kind of experiences over an extended amount of time to teach your dog how to interact with others. It's important that these lessons come early in a dog's life—some trainers say between months four and seven. This can be a lot of fun for you and your dog and doesn't have to feel like work. However, it is important that your dog interacts with lots of different animals and people in their early life.

Photo Courtesy of
Alexandria Campbell

Photo Courtesy of Cameron Warner

# Importance of Good Socialization

Imagine a world in which you have never seen another person before. One day, a scary human approaches you and starts acting in ways that seem strange to you. They might even yell in your face or put their hands on you in an aggressive manner. How might you react to this? Would you be excited to interact with other people, or would you have your guard up the next time you go outside?

This is sort of what a non-socialized dog experiences when they go out into the world. It's easy for a dog to become isolated when they only spend time at home with you and your family. However, it's important for your dog to have lots of good experiences with other people and animals. Sooner or later, your dog will need to leave the house. When this happens, you don't want them to be fearful or anxious. Frightened dogs are more likely to become aggressive in order to protect themselves. Unfortunately, someone can get hurt by a frightened dog. Pit Bulls are generally very gentle, but any dog will defend himself if the danger is great enough.

However, if your dog has a lot of good experiences around other people and dogs, he will be more likely to play and interact with others. This makes it possible to take your dog to training classes and dog parks, and just walk around city streets without worrying about your dog's behavior. You'll want to show your dog off to anyone and everyone, so you'll want to ensure your dog will be fine in all of these situations.

# Behavior Around Other Dogs

Pit Bulls are not known for their love of other dogs. Because of this, you want to make sure that your dog has plenty of safe and positive experiences to spend time around other pups. A puppy training class is a great way to introduce your dog to other dogs. Every dog in the class should be well controlled and on a leash, so there's no big risk of another dog scaring your dog. Plus, when all of the dogs are little and curious, your Pit Bull is less likely to become intimidated by the others.

A dog park can be a different situation. Here, dogs of all breeds and ages mingle. And, not all dogs are gentle with one another. If your Pit Bull is ambushed by a pack of rambunctious dogs, he might be a little wary of playtime with others. If your dog doesn't seem to like to play with others, perhaps it's best to visit the park when it's less busy, like early in the morning. This allows your dog to sniff around the other dogs without having to be surrounded by them. You may also try to find other

*Photo Courtesy of*
*Kierah Baker*

dog-friendly dogs to have play dates with. This way, if your dog gets annoyed, you can easily separate the dogs.

Socialization should be a process. First, introduce your pup to a few other dogs in a calm, controlled situation. Then, continue to raise the stakes until your dog is comfortable passing another dog on the sidewalk or can play in the park without an altercation or anxiety. With enough positive interactions, your dog will be playing with others in no time.

## Greeting New People

Socializing with humans should be no problem for your Pit Bull. This breed loves to hang out with people and adores attention. However, it's still a good idea to get your puppy used to being around all sorts of different people. Especially with adopted dogs with past lives, some people are a little more frightening than others, especially if your dog has had some bad experiences.

While some Pit Bulls may run up to a stranger and demand pets, some will be a little

**HELPFUL TIP**

**Great with People; Questionable with Animals**

Pit bulls are extremely friendly and sociable dogs and are great with children and adults alike. However, when encountering unfamiliar people or animals, especially in high-stress situations, they may become anxious and aggressive or have "temper tantrums" more frequently than other breeds. Therefore, try to make contact with strangers in calm environments.

more wary. After all, they want to protect their owner from any potentially dangerous foes. For this reason, it's a good idea to teach your dog that they can trust other people. Ideally, when someone approaches your dog, they'll offer a hand for a quick sniff. Once your dog feels a little more oriented, they'll approach the person or back away.

When you're teaching your dog to trust strangers, remember to use treats. Go on a walk and ask friendly strangers if they'll give a treat to your dog if he behaves nicely. Invite your friends over to give a peace offering to your dog in exchange for cuddles. Try to interact with all sorts of different people. You may find it silly, but sometimes dogs can be leery of someone based off of their physical appearance. Of course, if your dog tries to back away from someone, don't force them to interact. Instead, try again later when your dog is feeling a little more secure.

# Pit Bulls and Children

*Photo Courtesy of Zephan Tate*

Pit Bulls and children tend to get along swimmingly. However, it's important to be cautious when any dog is around a child. As stated in previous chapters, children do not always know how to behave around dogs. If a dog doesn't have a lot of experience with children, he may not understand why these tiny people are so loud and rambunctious. If your dog is already nervous, then gets a poke in the eye or their tail gets pulled, the dog might snap to defend himself. As an owner, you are responsible for your dog's behavior. If you notice your dog is getting upset, you must correct the children and calm your dog.

Of course, dogs are less likely to be nervous of something if they've already experienced the thing and nothing went horribly wrong. So, if your dog gets to run around and play with a bunch of children, the Pit Bull will probably have no problem with their loud noises and fast movements. If your dog has been poked and prodded and then cowered in fear, he may be less likely to agree to rough play from a child in the future. So, set your dog up for success by choosing early interactions that will not overwhelm your dog as they try to make sense of the world around them. Teach children how to properly pet a dog. Instruct them that the dog's head can be sensitive, but petting their back is okay. Over time, your dog will start to be able to handle a little more excitement and chaos.

# Educating Others about Your Pit Bull

Unfortunately, other people may fear your dog, even though you know that he's perfectly gentle and well behaved. Though it isn't your job to change public opinion on your own, you might consider your dog's unfair reputation when entering public spaces. For example, when approaching a stranger on a walk with their dog, let them know that your dog is friendly and ask if their dog is too. If they say yes, let the dogs sniff each other out. When out in public, encourage other people to pet your dog and let them see how friendly your pup is. At the dog park, introduce yourself and your dog to other owners. Maybe you'll meet new people who would be willing to advocate for Pit Bulls once they know how sweet the breed really is. Show people that they have nothing to fear when they see your dog walk down the street.

Pit Bulls are friendly toward people, but they still need socialization skills to become good doggy citizens. They are not always great with other dogs, but spending time around other canines in a controlled environment can ease their fears. If you want to take your dog out in public without issues, it's a good idea to do this socialization early in your dog's life. That way, you can share your dog with others and they can see for themselves how special Pit Bulls are.

# CHAPTER 8
# Pit Bulls and Other Pets

While some Pit Bull enthusiasts might say that Pit Bulls should not mix with other animals, with proper socialization, your Pit Bull doesn't have to be an only pup in your household. When it comes to different dog breeds, some are compatible with other dogs and some are less so. Pit Bulls are one of those breeds that are not known for being fantastic with other dogs. Still, with the right training and the right household, it's not impossible to have a Pit Bull that gets along with other family pets.

## Introducing Your Puppy

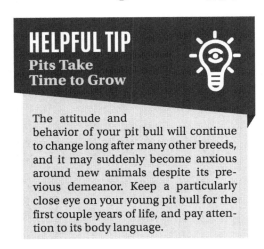

**HELPFUL TIP**

**Pits Take Time to Grow**

The attitude and behavior of your pit bull will continue to change long after many other breeds, and it may suddenly become anxious around new animals despite its previous demeanor. Keep a particularly close eye on your young pit bull for the first couple years of life, and pay attention to its body language.

First, you might want to consider how well your existing pets get along with other dogs before bringing a new one in. If you have a dog that growls when other dogs come near, then maybe it's not the best idea to permanently bring a new one home. But, if your existing dog is calm and friendly, you might have a relationship that works.

Puppies are incredibly malleable when it comes to teaching them new behaviors. If they enter into a situation where everyone is acting normal, they are likely to accept whatever is going on around them. If they're thrown into a situation that's scary, they might develop aversions. So, if your introduction experiences are calm and positive, then it's likely that many future interactions between your dog and other dogs will follow in the same pattern.

If possible, try to introduce your dogs in a neutral space before you get to take your dog home for good. These early interactions will tell you if these dogs are compatible. It's much better to find these things out before all of the paperwork is finalized and your dog is in your home for good.

*Photo Courtesy of*
*Corry Field*

# Pack Mentality

Photo Courtesy of Sierra Fulks

While some dog experts don't put much credence in pack mentality in domesticated dogs, others use it to explain why dogs act the way they do around other canines. It seems as though there is no clear answer as to whether dogs behave like their ancestors or not, so it may be helpful to understand why your Pit Bull acts a certain way around other dogs.

Canines are historically pack animals, meaning that they travel with others of their species. Within this pack, it is believed that there are different roles that make up a social order. The leader, or alpha, keeps the other dogs in line and makes the rules. From there, other dogs fall into their place in the social hierarchy. Some dogs will be dominant and whip the other dogs into shape, and some will be submissive and follow the rules.

Even though your dogs are not necessarily in a pack, they may show some of these traits. Some dogs are clearly more dominant than others. These dogs are quick to approach others and initiate play. Some are clearly submissive and may even roll over onto their back when approached by another dog to show that they are not a threat. This doesn't necessarily mean that one dog is aggressive and the other is anxious. It just means that these dogs have a different role in their "pack." And these roles can change depending on which dogs are interacting at any period of time.

You may notice that your dogs have a social order in your home. Maybe one dog has to eat before the other one. Or maybe one rolls over and surrenders during playtime. This is not something to be concerned about, as long as neither dog is harming the other. If the dynamic progresses to the point where fights are breaking out, then it's time to assess their behavior. Otherwise, it's fine to let your dogs be dogs.

# Fighting

When dogs begin to show aggression toward each other, it is vital for an owner to step in and break up the tension. A dog can do a lot of damage to another, even if it's generally friendly. Hopefully, you'll be able to recognize the signs of conflict before a fight occurs. If not, have a plan for breaking up a fight without getting hurt in the process.

Aggression generally comes from fear. Some of these signs include cowering, averting eyes, and tucking the tail between the legs. These fear signals can also be present in submissive dogs that are uncomfortable around others. Be concerned when these non-verbal cues change to ones that signal an impending defense mechanism. Growling, baring teeth, direct eye contact, and raised haunches are all signs that a dog is ready to use their fight response to get out of a scary situation.

If you notice any of these signs, separate the dogs immediately. Placing one in the backyard and keeping one in the house is a good option. This will give each dog a little space to chill out before they inevitably reunite. Or, you can always place dogs in separate rooms or different

Photo Courtesy of Tim Holke

crates. Make sure your dog cannot readily hear, see, or smell the other one in close proximity. When you bring the dogs back together after this cooling off period, keep a close eye on them, but try to stay relaxed. If you are worried about your dogs fighting again, they're more likely to be worried about it, too.

If things have progressed too far and the dogs are already fighting, do your best to split it up. Remember, a dog may turn on you, not because they want to hurt you, but because you're in the way of their fight. In the scuffle, they may not even realize that their owner's hand is in front of their face. Don't depend on your dog's affection for you to keep you safe in a fight. Your dogs may not even realize what they are doing.

There are a number of ways that dog owners break up fights, so you may want to have a couple of methods in the back of your mind if it becomes necessary to use one. One method that seems to work well is to pick a dog up by their hind legs and move them backward like a wheelbarrow. This keeps you out of biting range and allows you to disable the instigator by making it hard for them to fight. When your dog is away from the other, send them somewhere where they cannot come into contact with the other dog. Some owners, especially if they're without help, will stick some sort of barrier between the dogs, like a large baking sheet. This distraction will break eye contact for a short period of time

*Photo Courtesy of
Caleb Shofner*

and will probably startle the dogs as they are physically separated. However, whenever you place yourself between two fighting dogs, you open yourself up to the risk of getting hurt. You might also try the can of rocks method of correction, but if your dogs are locked in, they may not even notice a loud sound.

It's not unusual for dogs to squabble on rare occasions. Some of these conflicts can be worked out and then never brought up again. It's hard to know when a dog is going to feel particularly territorial about a toy or a favorite couch. When dogs are constantly fighting or causing serious harm to each other, it's become a problem. If you are unable to remedy this issue on your own, talk to a trainer or an animal behavioral specialist to help solve the conflict.

# Raising Littermates

If one puppy is great, two is better, right? While you may want to double the fun by getting two Pit Bulls from the same litter, you may want to reconsider. There are a few reasons why this is not an ideal scenario. For starters, it's hard to take care of two puppies at once. You're looking at double the supplies, double the expenses, and double the accidents in the house. It's hard enough to raise just one puppy. Taking care of two new puppies at once can be very challenging.

Even more important is the fact that littermates are difficult to raise, period. This is due to a strange phenomenon that some call "littermate syndrome." Puppies from the same litter often grow up to be codependent to the point where it can cause real trouble for you. When these puppies need to be separated, they freak out and become difficult to work with.

For example, let's say that one puppy has hurt his foot and you need to take him to the vet. If the dog gets separated from the other, the injured dog might make it very difficult for the vet to look at because he's panicking due to the separation. Meanwhile, the dog at home is tearing apart your belongings because he's upset that his brother is gone. Or, you pay lots of money to take both dogs to a training course, but neither dog wants to pay attention and learn important commands because they are distracted by the other. In fact, many trainers will prohibit littermates in their classes because they can be so disruptive to the class.

If you're in a situation where you've taken in littermates, try to keep them separated for short periods of time until they feel more comfortable being apart. Taking each dog for a separate walk may take a lot of time, but it will get your dogs comfortable with the prospect of being separated for a short period of time.

Photo Courtesy of
Sharna Wood

If you're really interested in having two Pit Bull puppies, consider buying dogs from different litters. Take one dog home and get all of the beginning training out of the way, then buy a second from that same breeder. That way, you'll have two similar dogs, but without that weird littermate bond that can make raising dogs difficult.

# What if My Pets Don't Get Along?

Maybe you've tried everything and your animals are still getting into fights every time you take your eye off of them. Perhaps you've even consulted with trainers and vets and you still can't seem to get everyone to love each other. If things aren't working out, you might be faced with a difficult decision.

If you haven't had the new Pit Bull for long, you might talk with the breeder about options for a refund. In serious situations like this, your breeder will want what's best for the dog. If you got your dog from a shelter or a rescue, they'll also understand that conflict happens, and they'll work to find a safe home for the Pit Bull. Or, perhaps you know someone who would make a great Pit Bull owner and does not have any pets in their home. These are all options that will put your pets in a good situation.

Avoid giving up your old pets for a new dog. If the puppy has only been in your home for a few weeks, it won't make a huge difference if he bounces to another home. A dog that's been with you for months or years will have a much harder time transitioning to a new home. Also, you don't want to do nothing and let the dogs continue to fight. If you're not working toward a solution that is best for every animal involved, this is abusive behavior. There is absolutely no shame in giving up a dog if that means that he will have a better life with another owner. It can be extremely difficult, but it's best to put your pets' safety and happiness first.

A full house of amazing pets can be a lot of fun, but it is not without challenges. Dogs can be unpredictable and live by a set of rules that is mind-boggling to humans. In order to make your pack as happy as possible, it's important to give your pets lots of time to become accustomed to one another. Pit Bulls aren't always compatible with other animals, so you'll definitely want to do a few trial runs before bringing your new dog home for good. If you've tried everything and you can't get your pets to get along, there is always someone else out there who will make an excellent owner to a good Pit Bull.

# CHAPTER 9
# Exercise

*"Pitbulls need a lot of exercise! If you don't own a home with a large yard, do not get a pit bull. They require 2 to 4 hours of daily hard playing to keep their mind at ease. I stress this fact to everyone: they are not apartment dogs!"*

**Edward Genther**
*Blue Passion Kennel*

Every dog needs exercise of some sort, but the Pit Bull needs a little more than most breeds. This is an extremely active and playful dog that needs an outlet for their energy. If this dog doesn't get the exercise they need, they will get bored and restless, leading to destructive behavior. Luckily, exercise can be beneficial to both dog and human. While your dog enjoys the fresh air, you'll be able to get some gentle exercise. Exercise can go way beyond walks, too. Before long, you and your dog will have a lot of fun activities to do while spending quality time together.

Photo Courtesy of
Annette Norman

Photo Courtesy of
Kathryn Rossi

# Exercise Requirements

The Pit Bull is generally not a couch potato. While some breeds can get away with just a short walk once a day, your Pit Bull will go crazy. Try to give your dog as much exercise and entertainment as you can throughout the day. While you might be able to tire your dog out in the short term, their energy will return later. When you settle down at night to watch TV and your dog paws at your leg to play, you'll wonder if you've done enough. In short, it's difficult to tire out a Pit Bull.

A nice walk in the morning will be the perfect thing for a Pit Bull. If they get anxious about you leaving for work, a little energetic output will help ease their nerves. And the entertainment will hopefully keep them from getting bored right away when you leave.

Later in the day, you'll want to partake in more strenuous activities. The afternoon can be a nice time for a longer walk or a quick jog. However, if you're a long-distance runner, remember that dogs aren't built to run extremely long distances. But a Pit Bull should be able to handle a mile or two. At least once a day, give your dog sufficient time outside to work out some zooms. Later on in the evening, you can burn the residual energy by more play-oriented activities like fetch or tug of war.

Though this breed is generally high-energy, every dog is different. If you're not sure how much exercise your dog needs, observe their behaviors. If your dog is rambunctious or even a little naughty at times, they can probably stand to have some more exercise. If they're totally pooped after a run and don't bother to get off of the couch for the rest of the night, then that level of exercise is probably sufficient. Also, if your dog is putting on extra weight, you may want to make sure your dog is being active.

Because Pit Bulls do not have a lot of fur to keep them insulated, they are susceptible to both overheating and freezing. When temperatures are warm, scale down on your outdoor exercise. Make sure your dog always has cool water and shade. If your dog seems to be very tired while doing your normal exercise routine, stop before your dog suffers from heat illness. For example, if you're on a walk and your dog suddenly stops and refuses to move, don't force them to run back home. Instead, find a shady spot and give your dog water until he's ready to move again. When it's extremely cold, consider dressing your dog in protective clothing while outside. If it's really cold, try to limit your dog's exposure to the elements.

# Different Types of Exercise to Try

Photo Courtesy of Sharna Wood

Pit Bulls are fun pets because there are so many things they can do. A nice walk or run is standard, but it's still very rewarding for a dog. Getting out into the fresh air to see new sights and smell new scents provides a lot of mental stimulation. While you may feel like you're doing the same activity over and over again, there's always something new and exciting for a dog beyond your yard. Even when the weather is less than ideal, keep this form of exercise in your repertoire.

If you have a spacious, fenced-in backyard or dog park available, Pit Bulls love to play games. Fetch and Frisbee are fun games to teach your dog.

They require your dog to run and jump, but also utilize important commands like "take it" and "drop it." Your dog will be having so much fun that they won't want to stop until they're positively exhausted.

Photo Courtesy of
Katie Royce

There are also lots of organized activities for your Pit Bull to participate in. Agility can be a lot of fun for Pit Bulls because it's a mental and physical challenge. After learning how to do all the different obstacles, your pooch will compete to complete the course faster than the other dogs. Even if your dog never participates in a formal competition, he can still practice running through the obstacles as quickly as possible.

If your Pit Bull is dog-friendly, you may also want to try fly ball. This is a sport that's like a doggy relay race. A team of four dogs complete a quick shuttle run with a ball before "passing the baton" on to the next dog. This is great for dogs that are bursting with energy. However, competitions can be pretty loud and crazy with so many dogs playing within a small area, so if your dog doesn't get along with others, then it might not be a great sport for him.

# Fun Games for Active Dogs

Intelligent, active dogs like the Pit Bull need just as much mental stimulation as physical. Sometimes, when the weather is less than ideal for going on a walk, you'll have to come up with fun activities inside to keep your dog's energy levels in check. Your Pit Bull might not be able to run up and down the hall as exercise, but there are a few fun games you can play with your dog.

Pit Bulls love to chew and they love to show off their strength. This makes a game of tug the perfect game for your dog. While some owners shy away from this game out of fear that it will make their dog more aggressive, as long as your dog isn't displaying any violent tendencies,

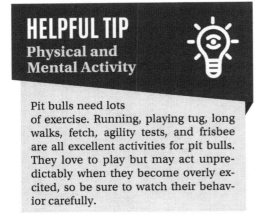

**HELPFUL TIP**
**Physical and Mental Activity**

Pit bulls need lots of exercise. Running, playing tug, long walks, fetch, agility tests, and frisbee are all excellent activities for pit bulls. They love to play but may act unpredictably when they become overly excited, so be sure to watch their behavior carefully.

there's probably nothing to worry about. However, when you play tug, always initiate the game and be the one to end it when you've had enough.

You may also use the skills you learn in dog training classes to entertain your dog. During the winter, lots of dog owners like to play hide and seek with their dog. To play, start with your dog in the sitting position somewhere where they cannot watch you walk to other parts of the house. Have them stay while you hide. When you're ready, call your dog to find you. They'll come running and sniff around different rooms until they locate you. Once they find you, reset and play until your dog loses interest. You can also hide certain toys and have your dog find them by name. This can be a challenging game for your dog that gets them off the couch and moving around.

If you're short on space in your home, a dog puzzle can keep your dog occupied for a while. There are lots of different puzzles on the market that use food to entice your dog to work at it. Kongs are popular toys because they're a simple rubber ball with a hole to stuff with oddly shaped treats. Your dog must figure out how to fling and bounce the toy around to get the treat to fall out. You can also fill the inside with peanut butter when your dog is overexcited and needs to calm down. There are other puzzle games that require your dog to nudge pawns, open sliding doors, and pull drawers in order to get the prize. There are different difficulties, so you can challenge your dog as they master different skills. Mental exercise is important for intelligent breeds like Pit Bulls.

*Photo Courtesy of Brendan Sloan*

Pit Bulls need lots of exercise, both physical and mental, to be happy and healthy. As the owner of a Pit Bull, you may have to find creative ways to keep your dog entertained. Walks and runs are a good place to start, but there are so many more fun things you can do with your dog at different times throughout the day. In between walks, try filling the extra time with games of fetch or Frisbee when the weather permits. If the weather or time of day

Photo Courtesy of Meredith Duncan

keeps you inside, try a few indoor games to get your dog's mind and body working. Giving your Pit Bull plenty of exercise is a way to show your dog that you love them and it's a great way to spend quality time with your dog.

# CHAPTER 10
# Training Your Pit Bull

*"It is important to understand that a Pitbull respects dominance, it must know its place in the household. If you have children they should be involved with the obedience training of your Pitbull or else the dog will run the house."*

**James Jackson**
*Flatline Kennels*

Photo Courtesy of Janet Ramos

It is so important to train dogs of any breed, but it is perhaps more imperative as an owner of a Pit Bull to ensure that your dog is able to follow your directions. Because Pit Bulls are often portrayed as aggressive and unruly, it might make you feel better to know that your dog is well behaved and well trained so no one can accuse your dog of being bad. Apart from that, it's a pleasure to have a well-behaved and responsive dog in your home. Pit Bulls are fairly easy to train because of their intelligence. It can be a lot of work to train a dog, but it's absolutely worth it when you have some control over your dog's behavior.

Photo Courtesy of Zephan Tate

## Clear Expectations

Especially with breeds like Pit Bulls, it's important to set clear expectations for your household and your pup. Pit Bulls are intelligent, but they might try to make their own rules if they aren't given clear guidelines for how to behave. You also want everyone in your household to hold your dog to the same standards for some consistency in your dog training. For example, if you use the command "off" when you want your dog to not jump on someone and another family member uses the word "down" for the same thing, you'll have some confusion. Also, you want your dog to respect each member of the home as the pack leader. For this reason, it's a good idea to get everyone involved with dog training so everyone is on the same page when it comes to your dog's behavior.

## Basics of Operant Conditioning

Training a dog is just simple psychology in action! If you're familiar with operant conditioning, you can apply these principles to dog training. If not, this chapter will serve as a lesson in psychological concepts, applied to dog training. In a nutshell, operant conditioning is creating consequences for your dog's behaviors, both good and bad. Over

Photo Courtesy of Melinda Hill

time, these responses will shape your dog's future actions in response to commands.

For example, if your dog sits, this is a desired behavior. If your response to this behavior is a tasty treat, your dog will want to do whatever it takes to get that treat again. With enough repetition, your dog will begin to automatically do the action at your command. After a while, they are not necessarily even doing the command for a treat, but because it's so engrained in their brain to sit when they hear your command.

On the other hand, dogs can also learn through negative reinforcements, or punishments. However, punishments often backfire on owners and produce even worse behaviors than the ones they were dealing with to start. A punishment can be any response you give to an undesired behavior. Dogs will learn to avoid behavior that results in a punishment, but that doesn't necessarily mean that they will behave in the way you want. Positive training is the best way to teach a dog how to behave.

In practice, operant conditioning in dog training can be pretty simple. Once you master basic training concepts, you can apply them to any command or trick you can think of. Training skills will be covered in a later chapter.

# Primary Reinforcements

When training your dog, you will probably use primary reinforcements as your main source of reinforcement. This is a reinforcement that is good in and of itself. Treats are a great example of a primary reinforcement because treats hold an inherent value to your dog. Food-driven dogs will do whatever it takes to get a tasty snack, including listening to your every word and watching your movements.

There are other types of primary reinforcements for dogs. Some dogs don't go absolutely wild for treats and prefer toys. If your dog fits this description, try finding a special squeaky toy for your dog to play with when he successfully completes a command.

If you decide to use treats, try to find high-value treats for your dog. Every dog has a different preference when it comes to food and treats, so test out a few flavors until you find one that your dog really loves. Consider saving the really good treats for training time so your dog also learns to love the time you spend together to work on commands. Moist, fragrant training treats or even little pieces of hot dog work well.

# Secondary Reinforcements

Secondary reinforcements are not inherently rewarding, but have value to a dog. Praise is a good example of a secondary reinforcement. Kind words aren't necessarily valuable on their own, but the meaning behind it is. When you praise your dog, you probably also give him pets or treats to show you love them. This creates the positive connection in their mind. If you call them a good dog after they sit, then they know that this goes hand in hand with a treat or a toy.

Another common secondary reinforcement used in dog training is a clicker. This is a small device that makes a clicking sound when you push the button. To teach your dog that the click is as good as a reward, you give treats in addition to making the clicking sound. Over time, your dog learns that the click is a good thing and you no longer need to give treats with the sound. This makes dog training simpler and more precise.

Secondary reinforcements are helpful tools to have in your disposal, along with primary reinforcements. As you start training your dog, you can experiment with different types of reinforcements until you find a system that works best for you. In the end, you want your dog to think that they're the best dog in the world when they do what you want. Dogs respond strongly to positivity, so if you keep training fun and rewarding, your dog will be more likely to do as you say.

# Dangers of Negative Reinforcement

Negative reinforcements, or punishments, are another part of operant conditioning. However, this type of reinforcement should only be done for extreme cases, under the supervision of a reputable trainer. Even then, negative reinforcement in dog training can produce undesirable effects and harm the overall well-being of the dog.

In the chapter about housetraining, the example of rubbing your dog's nose in the accident and shouting at them falls into this category. Yelling is a punishment because it makes your dog feel upset and afraid. While this may be a deterrent, it may just lead them to other issues. In the housetraining example, a dog that's afraid of using the bathroom around you because they're afraid you might yell could refuse to go potty on walks and have accidents in hidden places indoors.

If you swat or shout at your dog for making mistakes while training, they will likely come to hate dog training. When it's time to learn a new command, they're going to be too worried about their punishment to learn the new trick. Or, your dog will become so worked up that they'll completely avoid or resist training.

You may encounter common forms of negative reinforcement when it comes to training your dog. For example, shock collars use an uncomfortable sensation to keep your dog from doing certain behaviors, like barking. Though these methods are fairly commonplace, they are not necessarily right for all dogs. Pit Bulls are sensitive dogs and may react aversely to training methods that are meant to cause pain or fear. When in doubt, always give positive-only training methods a good try before even considering other avenues. It may feel like you're doing a ton of work for little reward, but persistent, positive training is generally enough for the average Pit Bull.

# Hiring a Trainer and Going to Classes

Dog training can be a lot of work and there are plenty of resources out there to help you and your Pit Bull. A training class is a great way to interact with other owners and other dogs. You'll also have access to a trainer that can help you with any of the questions you may have about your Pit Bull. This person will be a helpful resource not only while you're in the class, but afterward, too. Most trainers are very willing to offer advice, even after the course is finished.

Photo Courtesy of
Jamie Lee Hall

Or, if you'd prefer to have a private trainer, this is also a possibility. It is more expensive to hire a private trainer than to attend a group session, but if your Pit Bull is not ready to be around other dogs, this is a good option. Private training is also helpful if your dog has behavioral issues that you don't know how to fix on your own. A trainer can tailor their instruction to fit your dog's unique needs.

Your trainer does more than just train your dog. In fact, your trainer's job is to train the owner how to train the dog. Your class is merely just a space for you to work with your dog under the trainer's tutelage. There are tons of different classes to choose from once your dog has mastered basic skills. Once you finish one, try another and another until your Pit Bull knows every trick in the book.

When choosing a trainer, look for one that uses positive training methods. Ask for recommendations from breeders, vets, or other owners of well-trained dogs. Or, talk to your city's dog clubs and see what classes are offered. If you ever feel like the trainer does not have your dog's best interests in mind or uses negative tactics, find a new trainer that focuses on positive training.

## Owner Behavior

**QUOTE**
**Nature Versus Nurture**

"When it comes to influencing the behavior of an individual dog, factors such as housing conditions and the history of social interactions play pivotal roles in behavioral development."
The American Society for the Prevention of Cruelty to Animals (ASPCA)
https://www.aspca.org/

Many dog owners don't realize that their behavior affects their dog's behavior. Think of your dog's leash as a conductor of energy from you to your dog. If you're angry or anxious about your dog's training, your dog will feel that. If you're calm and positive, your dog will feel more comfortable and at ease. It may sound silly, but dogs use non-verbal cues to figure out what their humans want them to do. Pit Bulls are sensitive dogs with an acute sense for how their owner is feeling. If you're fed up, so is your dog. If you're positive and ready to learn, your dog is more likely to be, too.

Training can be a frustrating time for you. Dogs can be difficult to control because you don't share the same language to reason with them. So, if you find yourself getting frustrated to the point that you're noticeably angry at your dog, take a break. Come back to where you left off once you've had some time to cool down. Not only will it make training more enjoyable for you, but your dog will get more out of it when you're in a good mood. Training should always have positive elements in it, to the point where your dog is eager to learn more new things.

When it comes to training, you have to think like a dog. Any hope of reasoning with a Pit Bull goes out the window when working with your dog. Instead, use treats, toys, and praise to condition your dog to follow your command. Repetition is key here—keep practicing and rewarding until the behavior sticks. Once you've got the basics down, you can apply them to any kind of behavior. If you have issues with your training, don't forget that there are lots of training experts out there to help you. A class can be a fun way to bond with your dog while learning new training techniques. A professional trainer is also an awesome resource to have at your disposal in case you ever have questions about your dog. Training has the potential to be a lot of fun, but it can also be a ton of work. If you ever feel exasperated at your dog, take a break and come back to it later. Dog training should always be fun and positive for you and your Pit Bull.

## CHAPTER 11
# Dealing With Unwanted Behaviors

*"You have to respect your dog its strength and weaknesses. Understand what you Pitbull is and what it was bred to do. Dog aggression can present itself anywhere from 16 months to 2 years and sometimes can be corrected, but never assume. Once displayed you have to know your dog and not put it in a situation it's not comfortable with. They are not bad dogs, but keep in mind they have a strong prey drive."*

**James Jackson**
*Flatline Kennels*

As sweet as your Pit Bull may be, he probably won't be a little angel all of the time. Every owner has different standards for how they want their dog to behave. For example, some don't mind barking while others expect their dog to be silent while in the house. There are lots of behaviors that may be classified as unwanted. This chapter will help define these behaviors and give possible solutions so you don't feel as if you're constantly battling your dog's behaviors.

# What Is Bad Behavior?

Bad behavior is somewhat of a subjective term. What some owners will not tolerate, others will let slide. It's easy to think about how you want to deal with bad behaviors when you split them into categories. Bad behaviors can be seen as annoying, destructive, and dangerous.

Annoying behaviors are the kinds of things that some owners might tolerate, while others plan on enforcing strict rules. Barking is one of these behaviors. No one wants to come home at the end of a long day to a dog that barks at every little noise or movement outside, nor do the neighbors want to hear constant barking while you let your dog out. Another annoying behavior is when an excited dog jumps up on you to greet you. It's not polite for a dog to jump up on people, nor do you want dirty paw prints on your pants. It's a behavior that's probably not going to hurt anyone, but it's annoying enough to disrupt your life on a small scale.

Some bad behaviors cause damage to property, so you're probably more willing to correct them. Chewing is a big issue with Pit Bulls. They have strong jaws that can leave deep tooth marks in furniture. They are also smart dogs that chew to entertain themselves. If your dog is left un-attended in the backyard, he may decide to dig a few holes before any-one notices. This kind of behavior can leave unsightly divots in your land-scaping that can be a pain to fix.

Finally, there are some behaviors that are downright dangerous. If your dog gets nervous around humans to the point of aggression, it's imperative that you correct these behaviors before someone gets hurt. While this is rare with Pit Bulls, it's something to look out for if your dog has had a rough past. The same applies for dogs that don't get along well with other dogs. Aggressive behaviors should never go unchecked. You may also want to consider behaviors that could potentially be dangerous for you or your dog, on a lesser scale. If your dog pulls while you walk, this could cause injury to you. Or, if your dog likes to bolt into the street every chance they get, you'll want to figure out how to successfully recall your dog so he doesn't get hurt.

As a Pit Bull owner, you may have to make decisions about the behav-iors you will accept and the behaviors you will never tolerate. That way, you can start working on breaking bad habits, according to the severity of the behavior. Make any dangerous behaviors first priority. Once you get some of those issues sorted, you can work on the lesser annoyances.

*Photo Courtesy of Kristen Wood*

# Finding the Root of the Problem

Though it may seem as though there is no rhyme or reason as to why your dog does the things that he does, there's probably some rationale behind their actions. When your dog acts up, it's up to you to examine the situation and find the cause of the behavior. Once you find the triggers, you can work to desensitize your dog, teach new behaviors, or avoid the triggers.

**HELPFUL TIP**
**Don't Expect the Worst**

If an aggression or behavioral problem arises, focus on figuring out the problem, and not the misconceptions of the pit bull "breed." After all, pit bulls pass the American Temperament Test Society's temperament test as often as Newfoundland dogs, which are sometimes labeled as the best-behaved breed!

For example, you may notice that your dog barks incessantly every evening when you're trying to relax after work. Nothing you do seems to break your dog's attention and their noise is extremely annoying to you. Take a moment to assess the situation. When you take a step back, you may notice that you leave the blinds open on the windows that face the street. Your dog is clearly stimulated by something happening out there. And, once you look outside, you notice that the neighborhood kids are outside playing before supper. Perhaps your dog is alerting you to the fact that there are people outside of your house. So, once you figure out what your dog is yapping about, you can simply close the blinds so they can't see the kids, or you choose to walk your dog at that time so they're too tired and distracted to bark.

If you're dealing with a behavior like jumping up on people, this can be corrected once you understand the reward the dog gets for the action. When your dog jumps on someone, it instantly directs their attention to the dog. Also, the person may pet the dog because Pit Bulls are adorable and hard to resist. This becomes a reward for your dog. They learn that if they jump, someone will pay attention to them. So, to fix the problem, you must do the opposite of what they want. When they jump, turn your back to them. This will show that you will have nothing to do with this behavior and you won't unwittingly reward it. With enough practice, your dog will not even bother to try jumping on you because they know it won't go anywhere.

If you can start to figure out the reward your dog gets out of certain situations, it can make it easier to figure out how to correct the bad behaviors and reinforce the good ones. It can be difficult to think like a dog, but with enough observation, you may notice subtle clues that will lead you inside their brain.

# Bad Behavior Prevention

The best way to avoid constantly battling your dog's naughty behaviors is to prevent them altogether. However, this is easier said than done. If your dog has had a previous owner, you have little control of what your dog learned in their early life. So, the moment you catch these behaviors, you must put a plan into place on how to solve them.

If your Pit Bull is a puppy, training is key. You must spend a lot of time observing your dog, basically waiting for them to make a mistake. Then you can quickly correct the behavior before it becomes a habit. So, the first time your dog jumps on you, quickly turn your back. This way, you can never give your dog a reward for the annoying behavior.

Along with correcting bad behaviors, reinforcing good behavior may go a long way. If your dog has a tendency to bark, teach your dog a command like "no bark." This way, you're simply giving your dog treats when they are quiet, while saying the command and giving them praise. You can also avoid bad behaviors by teaching different ones. If your dog runs to the door and jumps on the visitor every time the doorbell rings, you can teach your dog to lie down on their bed whenever the doorbell rings.

That way, your dog is out of the way and in a prone position that makes it hard to bark and be excited.

Also, a bored, energetic dog tends to get into trouble more than a tired dog. If your pup is constantly getting into trouble, take a look at his daily exercise. Adding some extra playtime or another walk to your dog's day may help him calm down enough to behave while in the house. Also, if the issue is that your dog is chewing on your belongings, make sure you have plenty of better alternatives around for your dog to gnaw on throughout the day. You cannot expect to teach your dog not to chew on anything. This is one behavior where you must find a suitable alternative.

# How to Properly Correct Your Dog

Correcting bad behaviors can be tricky because in general, negativity does not work well on dogs. When training, you want to be as positive as possible. When teaching a dog how not to do something, a lot of owners have the tendency to yell or use other tactics to deter their dog from making the same mistake again.

When you catch your dog in the act of being naughty, call their attention to the behavior. Clap your hands loud enough to break their attention. Some owners swear by a can of rocks to shake when their dog is really in the zone. A sharp "hey" may also work. The key is to keep your voice at a tone that gets

*Photo Courtesy of Kade Peterson*

their attention, but is not angry. Once they're looking at you, you might say "no" and redirect their attention elsewhere. For example, if you catch your dog chewing on the legs of the table, get their attention, tell them "no," then give them a chew toy to gnaw on. This shows them that when they have the need to chew, they should direct it toward a more suitable option.

Photo Courtesy of Meredith Duncan

Correcting bad behavior is difficult because you cannot punish your dog after the fact. Just like with finding accidents hours later, you cannot clap your hands and correct your dog after finding your shoes tattered, especially when you don't know when the destruction occurred. For this reason, you have to be constantly supervising your dog if you hope to catch and correct any bad behaviors.

Pain and fear have no place in dog training when it comes to correcting bad behavior. This tactic will inevitably backfire on you. Dogs respond to fear with aggression, so it can be dangerous to you or others around you if you make your dog feel like they have no other choice but to attack. Also, a dog that fears you is not a friend, but a victim. A good dog owner does not hit their dog because their pup ruined the carpet. Instead, a good dog owner with control their frustrations, gently correct their dog, then clean up the mess and wait until the next opportunity to teach the dog. Pit Bulls are sensitive dogs, and even too much angry yelling will damage them.

## When to Call a Professional

If your dog's bad behavior is causing a serious rift in the relationship between you and your dog, or their behavior is downright dangerous, it's time to call in reinforcements. There are so many resources for you to use when things go wrong. You might talk to your breeder because they know Pit Bulls well. It's possible that they've experienced similar issues and can give you some helpful tips for working through them. A trainer is also a good resource for training issues. An experienced trainer has worked with a lot of different dogs from all walks of life. It's likely that they've helped another dog and owner with a similar problem and know exactly how to help you. If worse comes to worst, you may decide you need to hire a private trainer to come to your home and diagnose your dog's issue and help you work with your dog.

Dogs are great, but they sometimes do things that are not compatible with their owner's life. When it comes to your dog's behavior, decide how you want them to behave and stick to it. Some battles, like not having your dog jump on your bed, might not be worth the fight. Other behaviors, like growling at strangers, requires attention before it progresses. If your dog does something you don't like, try to figure out why they do that particular action. Once you find a motive, come up with a few solutions to try. Sometimes you need to teach a new skill, while other times, you adapt to avoid the trigger. If things progress and you don't know how to fix the problem behavior, call an expert. There are many people out there who have solved these problems with other dogs and can help you do the same so you have a happy life with your Pit Bull.

# CHAPTER 12
# Basic Commands

Training is a part of a dog's upbringing that is often ignored. An owner spends so much time teaching a dog not to destroy the house that it seems like too much work to teach commands. However, it is extremely important for dogs to learn at least the basics. This chapter will cover some training techniques and step-by-step directions for teaching your dog the basic commands.

## Benefits of Proper Training

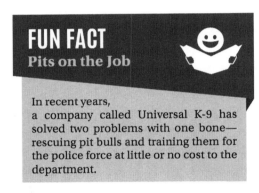

**FUN FACT**
**Pits on the Job**

In recent years, a company called Universal K-9 has solved two problems with one bone—rescuing pit bulls and training them for the police force at little or no cost to the department.

Obedience training is awesome for Pit Bulls. They are intelligent dogs that like to show off their skills. Training is a great way to stimulate your dog's mind. Oftentimes, intelligent dogs need "jobs" to keep them out of trouble. For a Pit Bull, his job may be to look after the kids and keep an eye out for strangers. However, if there are no kids to nanny, your dog might need a new job. Being told to sit, stay, or even retrieve specific objects will make your dog feel as though he has a purpose in your home. Mental exercise is much like physical exercise—if your dog is satisfied, he is less likely to participate in naughty behaviors.

Good training can also allow your dog to become a good doggy citizen. A well-trained dog minds his owner and pays special attention to verbal and non-verbal cues. So, when you're out in public, you can feel confident that your dog will be able to handle whatever you need him to do.

Also, training can come in handy in dangerous situations. If your dog is playing in the front yard and wanders out into the street, it's extremely important to be able to call your dog back to safety. Or, if there's an aggressive dog somewhere in the vicinity, you can have your dog sit right by your side and out of danger.

# Places to Practice

When it comes to training, the places where you practice matter. For instance, if you were to only practice commands in your house, your dog will become very good at sitting and staying in your kitchen. But if you take your dog to a restaurant patio and there are lots of exciting sounds and smells, your dog might be too distracted to obey. If your dog cannot sit still for your meal, then this can make things difficult for you.

For this reason, you want to practice your commands in as many different places as possible. At first, you may want

*Photo Courtesy of Stephanie James*

to stay in your house where you can control the distractions. But, after a few weeks, you might move training time to your backyard, then the front yard. Eventually, you can practice somewhere with a high level of distraction, like a dog park or a farmer's market.

Like with any other dog-related experience, it's best to start slow and work your way up to the most distracting location. If you start too big, you risk frightening your dog and having a generally frustrating training session. But, if you can master the commands in one location, it's great to challenge your dog by practicing in a new place. Don't expect your dog to be perfectly well behaved in a new place. Dogs have a harder time rationalizing different senses than humans, so they're bound to get distracted when a place has a different scent. Stay patient and keep working at it until your dog can be obedient in a place with a lot of distractions.

# Different Training Methods

*Photo Courtesy of Cameron Warner*

If your dog is food-driven (as many dogs are) you probably go through tons of treats. Treats make excellent rewards because your dog can smell the tasty snack in your hand and know what's at stake if they successfully complete the command. Rewarding a dog with tasty treats is highly encouraged because most dogs go wild for a yummy morsel.

But at some point, you may not have treats on hand, or you're overfeeding your dog. Also, if you give out treats for every successful exercise, your dog will come to expect it after every sit or stay, and may not perform if there is no treat. For this reason, it's helpful to have other markers that let your dog know that they are doing a great job. A clicker is a common tool used for dog training. This is a little device that makes a clicking sound when you push the button. First, you teach your dog that the click equals a treat. After you give treats while clicking the button, you can switch to using just the clicker. Because of the repetition and conditioning, your dog will see the clicker in your hand and do whatever you say so they can get a click.

If you don't have a clicker, it's a good idea to use sound cues anyway. Choose one short word to use when your dog does something good. "Yes" or "good" are excellent choices because they're short and easy to say. When your dog sits on cue, say "yes" along with the treat. If you're somewhere and you don't have any treats on hand, your dog will know they did something right when they hear you say "yes" in response to their action.

# Basic Commands

While there are so many commands to teach your dog, there are some that are possibly more important than others. The following commands can be considered life-saving because they can keep your dog safe and out of danger if a bad situation ever arises. These are some of the commands you'll see in a beginning training course, which are often prerequisites for more complicated commands. If you only ever teach your dog five commands, these are the ones to practice. Or, if you're hoping to teach your Pit Bull all sorts of commands, this is a good place to start. Once you master these skills, you can move on to more complicated commands.

## Sit

Sit is generally the first command a dog learns. It's an easy position for a dog to get into and it can calm your dog down enough to get them to listen to you. Many skills can be built upon sit, and it's a great way to teach your dog that if they do what you say, they get a reward. If you need your dog to chill out and wait for a moment, this is a good position to put your dog in.

To start, stand in front of your dog with them facing you. Take a dog treat in your hand and hold it in front of their face. This will grab their attention. Then, move the treat up and back toward their body, but not too far up or back. As you move your hand, your dog will slowly follow the treat with their

Photo Courtesy of
Jennifer Tonkin-Hulit

nose until they naturally sit down. When your dog's tush hits the ground, give them the treat.

Keep repeating this process until your dog understands what you're trying to get them to do. Then, begin to introduce the verbal cue. When your dog sits, say, "good sit" and give your dog the treat. Eventually, you'll say "sit" before introducing the treat. If your dog completes the command, give them the treat.

If your dog is having a hard time understanding what you want, you can put your hand on their bottom and push down with gentle pressure. This may be enough of a nudge to help your dog understand what you want.

## Lie Down

Once your dog is able to get into the sit position, you can teach the "down" command. This position is harder to get up from than the sit position, so if you need your dog to chill out for a longer period of time before springing back into action, this is a good command to use. You can also use it if you need your dog to go somewhere else and lie down, like on their bed or in a crate. This command is also the foundation for other fun tricks.

To teach this, have your dog sit facing you. Take the treat in your hand and hold it in front of their nose. Then, slowly draw the treat down toward the floor. Your dog will follow the treat with their nose until their belly is on the floor and their head is between their paws. When they hit this position, give them a treat.

This is not a natural position for many dogs. It may show submission, so dogs may be hesitant to get onto the floor. If you're having a hard time nudging your dog into the "down" position, you may want to practice using a collar and leash. As you move your treat toward the ground, gently pull the leash down with the other hand. This will apply gentle pressure to your dog's neck and shoulders. Hopefully, their entire body will follow their nose to the ground. Be careful to never force a dog into any position. This may hurt or frighten a dog that's already confused.

Once your dog can comfortably move to the down position, introduce the verbal command. As your dog practices this skill, try to get them onto the ground quickly by swiftly moving the treat from their nose to the floor. For an added challenge, see if you can get your dog to lie down from a standing position. It's tough to do, but it's a good way to increase difficulty of simple commands.

## Stay/Wait

Once you're able to get your dog into the sit or down position, you want them to be able to hold it. When you teach sit and down, it should be implied that the dog will stay in that position until he is given further instruction. However, there will be some instances where you'll want your dog to know that they're supposed to stay put. This command is useful when you need to walk away from your dog for a moment and you don't want them to move. A variation of stay, "wait," can be used if you want your dog to follow you out the door instead of bolting out in front of you.

To teach this command, start with your dog in the sitting position, facing you. Hold your hand out in front of your dog's nose like a stop sign. Take a few steps back with your hand extended, then come back to your dog. If your dog stays put, give them their reward. If they don't try again. As you work on this command, extend the distance as much as possible. You can also try going out of view or turning your back. For a dog that's very in tune with you, this will be very challenging. If your dog finds this difficult, you can try it with your dog on a leash. Drop the leash and stand on it when your dog tries to move. Once your dog starts to understand that they're not supposed to follow you, increase the distance and add distractions. Once the sit and stay is mastered, teach your dog to lie down and stay. This will also add another layer of difficulty.

## Come

Being able to recall your dog is extremely important. If your dog is off of their leash and they are particularly adventurous, you'll want them to come to your side on cue. This command is also useful when you're somewhere controlled, like the dog park, and you need to put the leash on your Pit Bull to take him home. This is one of those commands that can save your dog's life if something goes awry.

To teach this command, start with your dog on a leash. At first, a short leash will work, but you may want to buy a fifteen-foot leash once you step up your practice. Have your dog sit and stay, then walk away from your dog while holding the leash. Tell them to come and hold your arms out like you're about to welcome them into a hug. If they come running toward you, give them a treat and a ton of praise. You want your dog to think that following this command is the best thing in the world.

If your dog is distracted or hesitant, give their leash a gentle tug until they walk toward you. Place a hand on their collar as you praise them. If they stay for the pets, give them a treat. If they try to bolt before you can get a hand on them, try it again. Some dogs are playful and like to be chased. If you're ever in a situation where they get off leash and you need them to come to you, you'll want them to stick around long enough to get a grasp on their collar.

As your dog masters this command, raise the stakes. Get a long leash and practice sit and stay with distance, then recall them. Go to distracting places, like a park, and see if they'll still come to you when there are more exciting things going on. The ultimate goal is for your dog to drop everything and come running into your arms when they hear the come command.

## Leash Training

Because you'll be taking your dog on lots of walks, it's important that your dog is able to walk nicely on a leash. Pit Bulls are strong dogs and

*Photo Courtesy of Bruce Crow*

can pull you down the street if they have somewhere they want to be. Not only is this annoying, but it can be dangerous. A strong pull can injure an owner's shoulder and arm. If the conditions are slick, a quick jolt can send you to the ground. And, if you dislike taking your dog on walks because it's always a hassle, this form of necessary exercise may be omitted from the routine. So, for the best interests of everyone involved, good walking skills should be taught and reinforced from the very beginning.

To start, your dog should be on your left side with their shoulder in line with your leg. Hold the end of the leash in your right hand and slide your left hand down the leash to keep your dog close. The leash should fall slack between you and your Pit Bull. If your dog gets too far ahead, give the leash a gentle tug to remind your dog that they are supposed to walk with you, not the other way around.

It's important to keep treats on hand when you teach these skills. You might feel weird talking to your dog as you walk, but it can be very helpful when it comes to reinforcing good behaviors. As you walk, if your dog is by your side, give them tons of praise. If they look up at you as you walk, give them a treat. The key is to have your dog be as responsive to you as possible. Otherwise, a dog that's too focused on the road ahead of them is more likely to choose the direction and the speed.

If your dog is a puller, there are a few things you might want to do to get them back by your side. One technique requires you to turn around every time your dog pulls. This can get old after a while, but if you stick with it, it will show your dog that they are not the one in charge of choosing the direction. You might also try a harness with a front clip for the leash. With this type of harness, if your dog pulls, they will only cause their body to come right back to you, so they can't get to where they want to go. This is a good option for a dog that pulls so hard that they hurt their throat with regular collars. If your dog's pulling problem is serious, your trainer may suggest a prong collar. These collars make it extremely uncomfortable to pull on the leash. However, because they use discomfort as a training tactic, some owners and trainers are against using them. If you do use a prong collar, make sure you only use it as a last resort, you don't yank too hard on the leash and injure your dog, and that you give effusive praise after your dog self-corrects.

When you start leash training, you may just want to practice the basics in your living room or backyard. Then take a few laps around the block and make sure your dog stays by your side the whole time. As they get better at walking on the leash, take your dog to new places with new distractions. Once your dog has mastered the walking part, throw in turns, sits, and speed changes.

Once your dog has mastered these basic commands, it's time to move on to more challenging tricks. However, it's so important to continue to practice these basic skills. These commands make life with your dog so much easier and can even save their life in a scary situation. If you only ever teach your dog a handful of commands, make it the ones described in this section. However, you may find that you're having so much fun training your dog that you want to keep going! This is highly encouraged as dog training can be a rewarding experience for both you and your active Pit Bull.

# CHAPTER 13
# Advanced Commands

Once your dog has mastered a few key commands, it's time to work on more challenging tricks. Pit Bulls are active dogs with minds that need to be challenged. Continuing to train your dog after the basics are mastered can keep your dog entertained and help with their overall good behavior. There are so many tricks you can teach your dog, but this chapter will cover a few common commands that will help your dog become a good doggy citizen and entertain your family and friends.

## Leave It

This is a useful command if your Pit Bull is curious and likes to investigate everything. Your Pit Bull may want to stick their nose into anything that looks interesting, even if it's dangerous or disgusting. While it's nice to allow your dog to explore the world around you, sometimes you just know what's best for them. This command is useful if they are focused on something they shouldn't be, like a squirrel they want to chase, or a dead animal they want to use as puppy perfume.

To teach this, find a treat or a toy they go crazy for. Set it on the ground, with your foot nearby. Naturally, they're going to approach the reward so they can take it. When they get close, cover the treat with your foot so it's unavailable. Show them that they can't just eat any treat on the ground without your permission.

Try it again, asking them to leave it. If they dart toward the treat, tell them "no" and cover the treat. Repeat this until they appear uninterested or wait for the treat. If they successfully leave the treat, mark the behavior with a "yes" and give them the treat. This command should teach them to break their concentration when you tell them to "leave it." When your dog starts to get the hang of this command, you can command your dog to "leave it," then teach them to "take it." You may teach "take it" by giving them a release like "okay, take it" and making the treat or toy available to them. Now, you have opposite commands that can be useful in real-world situations, or when you're playing a game.

# Drop It

"Drop it" is a command that can save your dog's life if you catch them in a potentially dangerous situation. Dogs will put anything in their mouth. Sometimes the things they find are easy to choke on or will make them sick. This command will ensure that if you catch them with something they shouldn't have, they'll drop it instantly. Oftentimes, dogs know when they have a forbidden object in their possession, but don't want to give it up. When practiced thoroughly, your dog will give up their prize at your command.

*Photo Courtesy of Gianna Giordano*

This command can be taught during playtime as part of a fun game. Throw a ball and have them fetch it. If your dog doesn't automatically hand it over, this is the time to teach this skill. Many dogs don't understand that you want them to drop it so you can throw the ball again. As your dog stands in front of you with the ball in their mouth, show your dog that you have a treat. They'll want to eat it, but can't because there's already a ball in their mouth. If the treat is more rewarding than the ball, they'll drop the ball in favor of the treat. When they do this, say, "good drop it" and praise them. After a few tries, start using the command when they come to you with the ball. If they drop it when you ask, give them the treat and praise, then throw the ball again for an added reward. Once your dog has the hang of this, move on to different objects until they drop everything on command. As your dog gets good at this, raise the stakes with objects they really don't want to drop, like a new, tasty bone, or even a treat. If your dog is willing to let go of a treat, then you should feel confident that your dog would drop a dead animal when commanded to.

# Sit Pretty

Photo Courtesy of Tim Holke

There's nothing particularly useful about this trick, but it is very cute to see your Pit Bull sitting on their hind legs like a little human. If people are wary about your dog's breed, they won't be after watching your dog put on a cute performance. Along with this trick being absolutely adorable, it will help with your dog's core strength because it requires your dog to use muscles they usually don't need to engage. If your dog hasn't used these muscles a lot, then it's going to take some time to get used to sitting like a person. Your dog will probably be a little wobbly at first and you may need to give them a little support to keep them from tipping over. Keep practicing until they can hold the position.

To teach this command, have your dog start in the sitting position. Hold a treat in front of their nose, then slowly move it up and back behind their head. If they're following the treat with their nose, they'll naturally lift their body so they don't tip over backward. Reward them if they lift off of their front paws. Keep practicing until your dog can sit on their hind legs with their paws in front of their belly. From here, play around with other fun tricks, like having your dog go from sitting to standing as they balance on their hind legs. You might even try to incorporate a shake or high five once they get really good at balancing.

# Roll Over/Play Dead

Play dead/Roll over is another fun trick that doesn't have much of a practical use, but is a lot of fun for spectators. However, if your dog does not like to expose their belly to people, then this is going to be a challenge. It's not natural for every dog to feel comfortable in that position. If your dog is hesitant, keep trying, but never physically force your dog to roll onto their back. This may cause them to panic because they feel as though they're being forced to submit by a bigger and stronger animal.

Start with your dog in the sit position. Use the treat to guide your dog into the following positions: lower the treat to the floor to get them lying down and slowly rotate the treat around their head, until they lie on their side. Praise them and give the reward if your dog hits the desired "dead" position. For some, this is just a still dog on their side. For others, they like

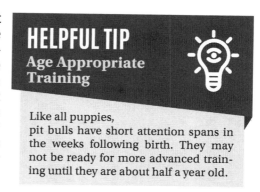

**HELPFUL TIP**

**Age Appropriate Training**

Like all puppies, pit bulls have short attention spans in the weeks following birth. They may not be ready for more advanced training until they are about half a year old.

their dog's legs to stick straight into the air. Some owners like to make a gun with their hand and say "bang" as the command word. Others like to say "dead dog" or "play dead." Your dog will respond to whatever cues you teach him, so feel free to get creative. Just make sure that whatever command you use is only a few syllables long and doesn't sound like another common command.

A "play dead" position is halfway to a "roll over" position. Instead of stopping the rolling motion when your dog gets to their side, continue rotating the treat for an entire roll. It may take some time until your dog is able to make a full revolution. But when he does, make sure to give your dog a ton of praise because it's a fairly challenging trick. As your dog gets the hang of this, try to work up some speed so your dog can quickly go through the motions without much prompting. Once you master one rotation, try to get your dog to turn the other way, too.

# Crawl

This is another fun and fairly simple trick that's easy to teach if your dog already knows basic commands, like "down." This trick may also be useful to practice skills that are used in agility training. To teach this command, start with your dog in the down position. Hold the treat between their paws, then slowly move it toward you. If you move the treat too quickly, your dog will probably go back up to standing. As your dog moves toward you, you'll have to back up a little so there's enough room for your dog to move forward. If your dog crawls a foot or two without standing up, give them their reward. Keep practicing to create more distance, and then try getting them to crawl without the use of the treat.

*Photo Courtesy of Alexandra Wassmer*

## Competitions for Pit Bulls

Competitions aren't just for show dogs. Any dog with the right training and temperament can participate in activities for dogs. Not only can competitions boost your dog's skills and self-esteem, but it's also a great way to socialize with other dogs and humans. Plus, it's a fun way to spend lots of quality time with your dog, doing something that benefits both of you. You'd be surprised at all of the fun things a Pit Bull can learn how to do.

Agility training might be a lot of fun for an energetic Pit Bull. This is basically just an obstacle course for dogs. Your dog will learn how to weave through pylons, run up and down ramps, and speed through tunnels. Focused Pit Bulls do well at agility because they're naturally driven and energetic. Your dog may not have the lean physique of other breeds that are built for speed, but competitions group dogs based by size. Even if you don't make it to competition, there are classes where you can learn and practice the skills just for fun.

If your dog is awesome at commands, obedience competitions may be your thing. These competitions require your dog to walk around a ring, sit, lie down, and stay, among other things. There are also more relaxed obedience competitions that allow you to freestyle and show off the fun tricks you've been working on with your dog. These competitions have an element of obedience around other dogs in close quarters, so if your dog doesn't love having a bunch of other dogs nearby, this might not be your thing.

Nose work is another dog sport that's becoming increasingly popular because it uses your dog's strengths to their advantage. These competitions allow your dog to identify and follow scents. Your dog doesn't have to be particularly athletic to participate, either. This is a good activity for an intelligent dog with a lot of mental energy. If your dog spends all of their time at the dog park with their nose in the ground, this might be fun for your dog.

There are so many fun things to teach your dog that can really make a difference in their day-to-day life. Not only will you have a better behaved dog, but you'll have a furry friend who enjoys the time that you spend with him each day, working on new commands. It takes a lot of work to teach your dog new and challenging things, but you'll notice an improvement in their behavior once you set a regular routine where you work on old and new commands on a regular basis. Finally, remember to keep training positive. Working on advanced commands should never be a drag. If your dog isn't getting something, there are always new commands to try. Keep building skills until there's nothing your Pit Bull can't do!

## CHAPTER 14
# Traveling with Pit Bulls

*"Pitbulls make great travel partners, because they always want to be with you.   They are the most human oriented dog I have ever been around.  I grew up with Samoyeds, Rottweilers and Dobermans, none of them are as intelligent or loving as a Pit and none of them had the willingness to always be at your side no matter what you're doing."*

**Edward Genther**
*Blue Passion Kennels*

Sometimes your life will take you away from your home for longer periods of time and you'll need to decide what to do with your Pit Bull. For some situations, it works best to take your little buddy along for the ride. Other times, it's easier to make arrangements for your dog to stay home with a trusted caretaker. Whatever the situation may be, you'll want to make sure your dog is fully prepared for whatever he will encounter during your travels. While your dog is away from home, you'll need to take precautions that will ensure that your dog stays safe and feels secure.

# Dog Carriers and Restraints

Just as you would insist that any human passenger buckle up while in your vehicle, it's equally important for your dog to be secure while you go for a ride. No matter how careful of a driver you are, accidents can always happen and they happen at the worst times. In the event of a crash, your unrestrained dog will continue to accelerate forward at the same speed you were traveling. Even at a low speed of twenty miles per hour, an abrupt stop can send your dog flying forward, potentially injuring him. At high speeds, an unrestrained dog may have a fatal injury and become a projectile that can hurt other passengers. Not to mention, a dog that is wandering around the car will inevitably pose as a distraction to the driver. All in all, there is no reason why a dog should not be restrained in your car.

Photo Courtesy of
Amanda Fields

There are a few different ways to keep your dog safe while traveling. If you have crate trained your Pit Bull, a crate can be a good way to keep your dog contained while traveling. Not only will it keep your dog from roaming freely, but it also has rigid walls that will help protect your dog from shrapnel in the event of a crash. Also, if the crate is a safe space for your dog, a nervous traveler may feel more secure while on the move.

However, if your dog has a big crate, it might not be so easy to transport your dog in his crate every time you go for a ride. There are relatively inexpensive seatbelts you can buy that clip into your existing seatbelts and attach to a collar or harness. These are just nylon straps, much like your own seatbelts, that will prevent your dog from flying forward in a crash. When using one, you may want to attach the seatbelt to a harness instead of a collar because of how the collar will pull on your dog's neck in a crash. A harness spreads out the force amongst the chest and shoulders, which are less fragile than your dog's neck. That way, if you have to brake suddenly, your dog is less likely to fly forward or get hurt.

# Preparing Your Dog for Long Car Rides

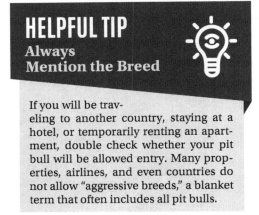

**HELPFUL TIP**

**Always Mention the Breed**

If you will be traveling to another country, staying at a hotel, or temporarily renting an apartment, double check whether your pit bull will be allowed entry. Many properties, airlines, and even countries do not allow "aggressive breeds," a blanket term that often includes all pit bulls.

Some dogs will hop in the car every chance they get, and some absolutely hate going for rides. One way to help your dog feel comfortable in the car is by teaching them that it's a fun place to hang out. This is done slowly and with lots of treats and encouragement.

First, let your dog explore your car before you get moving. Have him hop in and smell his surroundings. Give him a treat if he's calm and will let you clip him into the seatbelt. Once your dog feels comfortable getting into your car, start going on short drives, incrementally increasing the distance. Talk to your dog in soothing tones and act like you're having a great time. Before long, your dog will enjoy spending time in the car with you.

If your dog gets car sick, which is rather rare for dogs, you may need to figure out what the culprit is. In most cases, anxiety gives your dog that queasy feeling. If that's the case, work on finding ways to make your dog feel more safe and secure while you drive. Maybe you're the type to yell at other drivers while on the road and that frightens your dog. Or maybe your dog never had the opportunity to get acclimated to the car. If car rides only happen when going somewhere scary, like the vet, your dog will expect the worst when you get moving. Try to think like a dog and think of ways to make the car a happier place. If that doesn't work, you might talk to

*Photo Courtesy of Justin Rose*

your vet about your dog's symptoms and see if they can recommend medication or supplements that will settle your dog's stomach on a car ride.

Photo Courtesy of Matt Faupel

Sometimes your travels will take you on a long journey. When this happens, you'll want to make sure you're well prepared for everything your dog may need. You don't want to find yourself hundreds of miles away from home without your dog's supplies. Before you leave, make a checklist with your dog's daily essentials. Your car should be stocked with food and fresh water for breaks. Treats can comfort your dog in a new place, as can favorite toys or chews. A familiar blanket on the car seat may also make your dog feel more comfortable during a long trip.

During your journey, it's important to make frequent stops for your dog to get out and stretch his legs. While you may be able to drive five hours without stopping, that's a long time for a dog to be in a car without any breaks. It will extend your drive time, but your dog will be much happier if you give him the opportunity to go to the bathroom, have some water, and walk around. Before you leave, try to plan out rest stops in areas that have room for your dog to roam. Interstate rest stops often have large, grassy areas for walking dogs, but if your dog is skittish, the loud interstate noises may startle him. If possible, find a town with a dog park along your journey and let your dog have a little fun before getting back into the car. As an added bonus, your dog won't have so much pent-up, nervous energy when you get to your destination.

When taking your dog to a new or unfamiliar place, make sure your dog has proper identification in case your dog gets spooked and runs off. Along with a microchip, a collar tag with your contact information can help you find your dog in case of emergency.

Photo Courtesy of
Justin Rose

# Flying and Hotel Stays

Sometimes your travels with your dog might require you to put your dog in unfamiliar places. When you're covering a long distance, or taking your dog overseas, air travel may be necessary. However, this is best done in extreme circumstances where driving to your location is not feasible. Air travel can be hard on a dog and you don't want to put your dog in a risky situation unless it's necessary.

For starters, you'll likely be separated from your dog for quite some time. Airlines have restrictions about which animals get to fly in the cabin. A big Pit Bull probably won't make the cut and will be required to fly in the cargo hold. This area is loud, not always temperature controlled, and if it loses pressure, there may be nothing you can do about it. If you're on a long flight, your dog will have to stay in his kennel for hours without attention, reassurance, or bathroom breaks. And, just like any other piece of luggage in the cargo hold, your dog may become lost if mishandled.

This is not to say that these horror stories happen on a regular basis, but it is a possibility. If you must fly, there are a few things you can do to improve your chances of a problem-free flight. First, take your dog to the vet for a checkup prior to your trip. Tell your vet that you're planning on flying and want to make sure your dog is in good health. Next, make sure that there is plenty of identification on both your dog and your dog's crate. Label your crate with your contact information and your flight information in case your dog gets mishandled. Also, do some research before the flight and obtain the contact information of the airline representative you would need to speak with if your dog was to become lost. Finally, make sure your dog has food and water available for a long flight, along with a comfortable blanket to cuddle up with in case the cargo hold is too cold. While you are at the vet, ask if there is anything else you can do to make your dog more comfortable.

If you're staying at a hotel, you'll want your dog to feel secure and entertained enough that they won't destroy your room or keep your neighbors awake. If possible, try to find a hotel in an area that has some grassy space or trails nearby for walking your dog. In this kind of situation, it's important to keep your dog entertained and worn out.

When booking a hotel, make sure your dog is allowed. You don't want to arrive at your hotel, only to be turned away because of your dog's breed or size. Some cities have ordinances that do not allow Pit Bull breeds or place restrictions on their restraints. Brush up on the local legislation before you travel.

# Kennels and Dog Sitters

Perhaps it's just too much stress to take your dog on your travels because you know your dog wouldn't get the attention and care they need. If this is the case, you'll have to find a trusted caregiver for your dog. When it comes to hiring someone to take care of your dog while you're gone, you can either take your dog to a kennel for around-the-clock supervision, or hire a sitter to come to your house.

Kennels are great if you're worried about leaving your dog at home, where they get lonely easily or get into trouble. There, your dog will have their own little space to be alone, while also having the opportunity to go on walks or play in open areas with other dogs. However, this might not be the best option if your dog is easily agitated or fearful around other dogs.

A dog sitter can either come to your house or they can take your dog into their home, depending on the services they provide. This is great for dogs that get nervous around other dogs and feel safe in their own homes. If possible, try to find a sitter that can either spend large chunks

*Photo Courtesy of Anthony Corda*

of the day in your home, or someone who can make frequent visits. Your Pit Bull will need a sitter that can just hang out and keep your dog company, not just let your dog out to use the bathroom and go on a walk a day. Pit Bulls need plenty of love and affection, so choose someone who can spend a little extra time with your dog.

Before hiring anyone to take care of your dog, collect as much information about them as you can. If you're choosing a kennel, visit the facilities and see how the dogs are cared for. Ask the boarder any questions you have and voice any concerns about your dog's care. With both kennels and sitters, recommendations and client reviews can make you feel better about leaving your dog with a stranger. Don't be afraid to ask your dog's caregiver questions about their experience with dogs or request that they send you frequent updates during your trip. It's important that you can freely communicate with the person who will be in charge of your best friend while you're away.

When you're traveling and you have a dog, things can be stressful. However, with preparation, you can make your journey easy for both you and your dog. Even if the extent of your traveling is a drive to the vet or the dog park, you'll want to make sure your dog is safe and happy during your trip. While convenience is nice when it comes to longer trips, your number one priority is your dog's well-being. If you can't ensure that your dog will be safe or comfortable during your travels, you may want to find a suitable alternative to leave your dog at home. A happy dog can make a trip so much more enjoyable, so don't forget about your furry friend when making travel plans.

# CHAPTER 15
# Grooming Your Pit Bull

If you're looking for a low-maintenance breed when it comes to grooming, the Pit Bull is the right dog for you. Their short coat is easy to clean when your dog inevitably gets dirty. Even though this dog is easy to keep clean, there's more to dog hygiene than bathing. To keep your dog looking and feeling fresh, it's important to keep up with nail trimmings, tooth brushings, and ear cleaning. This can be difficult to do if you have a squirmy dog, but if you start these jobs early and make them positive, your dog will have no problem sitting still for a few minutes to get cleaned up.

## Coat Basics

Pit Bull breeds have a very short, straight coat. Unlike other breeds, this dog's coat is not in danger of becoming tangled and snared. So, don't worry about buying brushes with long bristles. However, it's nice to go over your dog's coat with a natural or synthetic bristled brush. Brushing is good for keeping your dog's fur clear of debris or dead fur. It can also distribute natural oils in the skin and fur that make your dog look sleek and shiny. So, even though you're not working with a long coat, regular brushing will still improve the look of your dog's coat and make them feel more comfortable.

Photo Courtesy of
Caleb Shofner

Photo Courtesy of
Paula Smith

# Bathing

Pit Bulls are active dogs that don't mind getting dirty. When this happens, you'll want to have a few things on hand to make cleanup easier. It's best to have some supplies ready before you need them; otherwise, you'll have to find a way to keep your house clean while you scramble to get supplies. First, you'll want a good dog shampoo. Choose one specially formulated for dogs, as human shampoo may cause a reaction with your dog's skin. A gentle solution is best, as to not strip too many natural oils from the skin and hair. Some dogs have sensitive skin, so if your dog is prone to allergies, pick a shampoo designed for your dog's sensitive skin. A detachable shower hose can make your dog's bath so much easier and cleaner for your bathroom. If your Pit Bull hates water, keep a few treats on hand use as positive reinforcement. Even if your dog tolerates the bath, you'll want to make the experience positive so your dog will continue to cooperate.

To start, fill the tub with a few inches of warm water. Even if you're using a hose, a soak will loosen all of the dirt in your Pit Bull's paws and nails. Give your Pit Bull a quick rinse and then work their fur into a lather with the shampoo. Pay special attention to their face to ensure that no soap or water gets into sensitive areas. It's best to use a damp rag on the face and save the soap for the rest of the body. Give your dog a thorough rinse when you're done. Any excess soap will dry out their skin and make their fur dull and their skin itchy. Once finished, towel dry your Pit Bull and give them a treat to reinforce the idea that baths are not so bad.

If your dog detests baths and squirms too much to get a good clean, put a little peanut butter on the back of the shower wall. This will keep them busy licking for a few minutes while you give them a wash. You might also make sure that the water isn't too hot or too cold, so they don't associate baths with feeling uncomfortable. While you may want to keep your dog super clean, dogs only need a bath once every few months, unless they're particularly dirty. Otherwise, you're taking away the natural oils that protect their skin and coat. If your dog is looking a little dusty, but has been bathed recently, take a damp cloth and wipe the fur clean. If your dog likes to get into stinky things, pet stores make scented wet wipes that can be used in a pinch.

## Trimming Nails

While you may not notice it until your dog gives you a scratch, nails should be kept trimmed. Not only do they click and clack on the floor, but they scratch people and furniture. And, if toenails grow too long, they can cause foot pain. Nail trimming is something that can be done at home, but dogs don't always sit patiently and wait for you to cut their nails. In fact, many dogs will resist having their nails trimmed and will try to avoid you when they see the clippers in hand. Before you even begin to cut nails, practice touching your dog's paws and work up a trust between the two of you. If they tolerate you touching their paws and nails, give them a treat. This will create a positive association between touching paws and yummy snacks.

When it comes time to trim the nails, don't try to cut too much off at once. Clip the nails with tiny snips instead of taking off big chunks to avoid cutting through the quick. Some dog nail clippers have guards on them so you don't take too much off. If you cut too much, you might nick the blood vessels in the nail. This can be extremely painful, will bleed, and will make your dog hesitant to let you clip them again. If your Pit Bull is too squirmy and you don't feel confident in your ability to cut nails, this is a service that a groomer can help you out with. They have lots of experience with a variety of dogs and can get the job done quickly for a low price.

# Brushing Teeth

Brushing your dog's teeth is about more than keeping their smile pretty. It also reduces bad doggy breath and removes harmful plaque from teeth. The condition of a dog's teeth makes a big difference in their overall health. When the teeth begin to decay, it makes it painful for your dog to eat. The bacteria from the decay can cause health complications. Bad teeth have been linked to heart disease, and can even take years off of an otherwise healthy dog's life. A lot of owners overlook dental hygiene because not a lot of people connect gum health to heart health, but there's definitely a relationship.

**HELPFUL TIP**
**Manage Mange**

Mange is one of the most common dog skin problems. Some pit bulls are especially vulnerable to mange due to having a weaker immune system. While grooming your pit bull, pay close attention for signs of mange, such as excessive hair loss or skin irritation. Early treatment can especially save older pit bulls from extreme discomfort and lasting health issues.

It may seem like a lot of work, but brushing a dog's teeth is not difficult or time-consuming. Before you begin, practice touching your dog's mouth to get them used to the strange feeling, just as you did with your dog's paws. Gently pull their lips back and poke at their teeth. This is also good practice for visiting the vet, because they'll check teeth in the same way at your regular checkups.

When they're comfortable with you touching their teeth and mouth, it's time to brush! Use a toothbrush and toothpaste made for dogs, not the same toothpaste you use. Dogs can't spit out toothpaste with fluoride, so they need a special formula that their body can tolerate These kinds of toothpastes come in a variety of dog-friendly flavors, like peanut butter. You can decide which type of brush to use, depending on the size of your dog's mouth and your comfort. There are traditional handled toothbrushes in a variety of sizes or rubber-bristled brushes that slip on over your finger.

When brushing, focus on the outsides of the back teeth. When your dog eats crunchy foods, the kibble scrapes plaque away from the inside parts of the mouth. The outsides tend to collect more of that plaque buildup that leads to disease. The insides and tops need a light brushing, but these parts tend to stay cleaner than the outsides. Gently brush your Pit Bull's teeth, taking care not to injure the gums with harsh brushing. Gentle circles will do the job.

The more frequently you brush, the better your dog's teeth will be in the long run. Some owners are diligent about brushing every night before bed, while others get around to it once a week. Prevention is key when it comes to your dog's teeth and the earlier you start brushing, the better. If you can keep your Pit Bull's smile white and shiny, then they'll be less likely to need professional cleaning from a veterinarian in the future.

# Cleaning Ears

Photo Courtesy of Donald Baker

When moisture and bacteria get trapped inside a dog's ears, they become a breeding ground for nasty infections. When left untreated, this can cause a lot of pain and potential hearing loss in your dog. Pit Bulls tend to have short ears, so this isn't as big of a concern as it is for floppy-eared dogs, but it's still good to keep them clean.

First, take special care to keep water out of your dog's ears. In the bath, don't rinse their face with the shower hose or dump water on top of their head, if you can help it. Some owners even place cotton balls in the opening of the ear to prevent water from going in. These cotton balls can then be used to gently wipe away grime.

If you notice that there's a lot of waxy buildup in your dog's ears and they're scratching and shaking their head a lot, it might be a good time to clean their ears. If your dog has allergies, they may need some extra cleaning to get irritants out. Pet stores sell ear cleaning solution that's safe for your dog. To use it, squirt the solution directly into the ear. Then massage the outside of the ear, working the solution down into the ear canal. This liquid will work to break up the wax in the ear. Let your dog shake the extra moisture out and you're good to go! If there's a lot of wax on the ear flap, you may use a moistened cotton ball to gently wipe the residue away. Never use Q-tips or any other small implement to clean deep inside the ear, as this can damage your dog's delicate inner ear. Keep in mind that it's jarring to have cold liquid squirted forcefully into your ear canal. This is another situation where it's best to use lots of positive reinforcement.

Of course, if your dog appears to be itchy or in pain after a cleaning, schedule an appointment with a vet. They can diagnose infection and prescribe medication to help with your Pit Bull's floppy ears. They will also clean their ears if this is too big of a task for you. Many dogs dislike the sensation of something cold and wet squirted in their ear, so don't feel bad if you can't get the job done. Sometimes it's best to leave the important tasks to the professionals. After all, it's better that the job gets done by someone than no one at all.

# Home Grooming vs. Professional Grooming

If grooming is not your thing, you can always outsource this job to the professionals. If you have an active, wiggly dog, you may risk injuring your Pit Bull with sharp objects like nail clippers. Professional groomers have a lot of experience and can handle anything that comes their way.

On the other hand, grooming can be expensive and it may be hard to find the time to take your dog in for an appointment if you just need to trim a few long nails. Because Pit Bulls are low-maintenance dogs, you probably don't want to make regular appointments for just baths. However, if cost is not an issue, go ahead and let someone else do the dirty work. Still, keep grooming equipment on hand in case you ever need it. But if you truly feel uncomfortable doing these tasks, leave it to the groomer. It's not worth injuring or traumatizing your dog if you're not able to do something yourself.

Consider yourself lucky that your dog is so easy to keep clean. For the most part, a quick wipe-down will keep your dog smelling and looking clean. Keep baths to a minimum to avoid drying out your dog's skin, and run a brush over your dog's coat every once in a while. Don't forget to regularly clip nails and brush your dog's teeth. This will keep your dog healthier in the long run if you keep up with it before it gets unmanageable. Again, if you feel as though you are unable to complete these grooming tasks, don't be afraid to have a groomer or a vet take over.

*Photo Courtesy of Harley Gonzalez*

# CHAPTER 16
# Health and Nutrition

There is nothing more important than our dogs' health and happiness. When you bring your Pit Bull into your home, they immediately become family. These dogs are so sweet and loving, it's understandable that you want to give them whatever they need to be happy and healthy. However, it's hard to know exactly what your dog needs. This chapter will cover good nutrition and healthcare issues that Pit Bulls occasionally face. That way, you'll be able to help your dog live a long and healthy life.

## Importance of a Good Diet

Photo Courtesy of Kathryn Rossi

It's a common misconception that dogs can eat anything. While your dog may eat a lot of questionable items, it doesn't mean that they should eat anything. Just like with any other animal, food is a source of fuel. If you feed your dog nutritious food, they'll have lots of energy and their body will work efficiently. If they eat junk, their bodies will not get the important things they need. Extra fat will accumulate around organs, causing them to work harder to function normally.

Dog food formulas tend to fit into big dog or small dog categories. A big dog can stand to have more carbohydrates in their diet because they burn more energy. Smaller dogs tend to need foods a little higher in protein. However, all dogs should be eating foods with good sources of proteins and carbohydrates.

When it comes to protein, multiple meat sources can provide a better range of amino acids and fatty acids. Red meats, like beef, tend to be higher in iron, while fish contains healthy fatty acids that are good for skin and coat health. Pit Bulls have a lot of muscle, so their food should be relatively high in protein to keep their muscles in good condition. However, they do not need supplemental amounts of protein, unless recommended by

**HELPFUL TIP**
**How to Care
for Your Pit Bull**

Pit bulls should get meals high in protein, moderate in fat, and low or lacking carbohydrates. The right diet will help prevent against common health issues like hip dysplasia, heart disease, and allergies. Be sure to avoid foods containing corn, wheat, and potatoes as many pits are allergic to these ingredients.

a veterinarian. Oftentimes, Pit Bull owners want their dogs to look as bulky as possible, possibly so they appear tough or imposing. However, there is no reason for average Pit Bulls to put on bulky muscle. If you're worried that your Pit Bull isn't getting enough protein, talk about your dog's diet with a vet. They can help you decide if your dog is healthy, based on nutritional recommendations, rather than appearance.

Carbohydrates is not a dirty word when it comes to your dog's nutrition. While their canine ancestors probably ate a diet composed primarily of meat, some carbohydrates are perfectly healthy in your domesticated pup. Complex carbs are good at keeping your dog energized and full for longer. Ingredients like oatmeal, brown rice, and barley will keep your dog's stomach from growling between meals.

Also, don't be afraid of fats in your dog's diet. Fat and oil are what keep your dog's skin moisturized and their coat smooth. Look for foods that have Omega fatty acids, like from fish oil. These nutrients are great for the skin and also promote healthy brain activity. A dog food with fat in it will not necessarily make your Pit Bull fat. A diet with little fat will result in a hungry, dull dog.

We all know that fruits and vegetables are good for people, but many don't consider all of the vitamins and minerals dogs need in their food. There should be a wide variety of vitamins and minerals at appropriate levels in your dog's diet. Almost all commercial dog foods contain some sort of multivitamin mix, but some contain the actual fruits and vegetables they come from. Real produce contains antioxidants that fight the aging process and may keep the immune system healthy. These fruits and vegetables also contain fiber, which keeps your dog's bowels regular.

Also, when it comes to feeding your dog, use the feeding guide on the bag to figure out how much they need per meal. The guide will tell you how much food a dog needs by weight. It's nice to have an accurate weight for your dog; otherwise, they might get too much or too little food. Because there can be a lot of variance in size between the different Pit Bull breeds, there is no standard recommendation for the whole breed. Feed your dog based on their weight, then increase or decrease calories, depending on how active your dog is.

# How to Choose Your Dog's Food

Now that you know what nutrients your Pit Bull needs to be fit and healthy, it's time to choose a food. This can be overwhelming when you go to the pet store and see the numerous options for your dog. Each brand has different qualities and price points, and comes in a wide variety of flavors. Before you go to the store, it's good to collect a little information and narrow down what you're looking for in a dog food.

If you're buying your dog from a breeder, ask your breeder what they use. This will give you a good idea of the quality of food Pit Bull experts use, and also tells you what your new puppy is used to eating during the weaning process. Sometimes dogs can be picky when it comes to flavors. If you don't know what kind of food piques your dog's interests, many stores will offer free samples of kibble to try.

You'll also notice that food comes in wet and dry varieties. The wet foods contain moisture, which makes the food more fragrant, thus more appetizing to a dog. However, it sticks to the teeth, leading to dental issues. This kind of food is easy for dogs with mouth issues to eat, but is not really necessary for a healthy dog. Crunchy food, on the other hand, scrapes the plaque off of teeth every time your dog chomps down. For this reason, it's best for dogs to eat dry food, as to limit the amount of plaque that develops on your dog's teeth.

Another thing you'll notice in the dog food aisle is that there's a wide variety of prices. Cheap dog foods can keep their prices low by using lower-quality ingredients. You can expect a lot of animal byproducts and cheap grains. Expensive dog foods often use ingredients that are closer to what people might eat, yet they're not technically human-grade foods. Also, a high price may signal to dog owners that it's a superior product, which may not always be the case. When in doubt, start by examining food labels in the middle of the price range. If the nutrient levels and ingredients look good to you, then it's probably a good dog food.

Also, while you want the best foods for your dog, don't be scared away by gross-sounding ingredients like chicken meal, organ meats, and cartilage. While this doesn't sound appetizing for a human, it's perfectly fine for a dog. In fact, there are compounds in animal joints that are helpful for your dog's joint health. So, just because it sounds like the dog food company is just using discarded bit of animals, it doesn't necessarily mean that they are not nutritious for your dog.

# Homemade Food

Some dog owners make their own dog food instead of buying commercial brands. This may be because they fear that dog food companies don't have their dog's best interests in mind, or because they believe that domesticated dogs should have a diet that mimics a wild dog's. While homemade foods are not the norm, it's sometimes beneficial for dogs. Occasionally, dogs will have food allergies and intolerances to certain ingredients, making it hard to find a food for your pup. Other times, owners don't like the idea of their dog eating anything lower quality than what they would feed their human family. In any case, making homemade dog food should be done under the supervision of a veterinarian or pet nutritionist to ensure that a dog is not missing any vital nutrients. These experts can recommend recipes and calculate caloric needs. There are tons of websites out there with owner-created recipes for inspiration, but be cautious of whom you trust. While dog enthusiasts on the Internet may love their dogs, many are not experts and eschew conventional science. When in doubt, always ask a vet first.

Photo Courtesy of Norma Vigil

# Weight Management

Just like with humans, dogs can become pudgy if they don't have the right balance of calories and exercise. While conventional wisdom would prescribe a calories-in-calories-out approach to weight management, it can be hard to figure out just how many calories your dog ingests in a day, as opposed to how many they burn. If your dog is overweight, according to a veterinarian's standards, you will probably reduce food intake and increase exercise. If it's still not working, there might be other issues at hand. Many owners forget about adding in the calorie contents of training treats. Especially when you're training, dogs can go through a lot of snacks. If these snacks are high in calories, the pounds will pack on quickly. Try to switch to a low-calorie treat, use berries or leafy greens as treats, or even switch to clicker training. It's also important that an overweight dog does not eat table scraps. When having guests over, make sure they know not to sneak any contraband to your portly puppy.

*Photo Courtesy of Joselyn Herrera*

# People Food

Some owners like to feed their dog bits from the table, while others completely prohibit it. Dogs love to eat table scraps and any other tasty treat they can get but it's not necessarily good for their bodies. When it comes to people food, it's best to err on the side of caution. First of all, you don't want to make your dog sick because your food contained something toxic to dogs. Onions, grapes, avocados, and chocolate are just a few things that humans can eat that make dogs very ill. Some foods, like dairy products, are not necessarily toxic, but your dog may not be able to digest them, leading to tummy aches and diarrhea. Also, if your dog is already eating a balanced diet, adding high-calorie globs of fat from your steak trimmings will pack on the pounds over time. Finally, if you teach your dog that they can have the occasional scrap from your dinner table, they're going to sit under the table and beg every time you eat. This will become extremely annoying and it's hard to break that habit once it begins.

On the other hand, some owners like to use people food as training treats because they can be nutritious and they're high value because they're rare. Some dogs go wild for leafy greens, berries, and cooked pumpkin. These are great for dogs because they are low calorie and packed with nutrients. As long as you use these as special treats and don't scrape them off of your plate, it's fine to feed these to your dog on special occasions. But, before introducing a new food, do a quick search to see if it is helpful or harmful for a dog's body. Then introduce it in small amounts. You don't want to have your dog load up on a new food, only to find that it doesn't agree with their tummy.

# Checkups and Preventative Healthcare

When it comes to your dog's health, it's best to prevent any issues before your dog becomes sick. One way to do this is to take your dog to the vet for a yearly checkup. During this time, they'll ask you if you've noticed any changes in your dog's overall health or ask if you have any concerns. Even if your concerns turn out to be nothing, it's still a good time to ask any questions you might have.

During your appointment, your vet will do a quick, but thorough examination of your dog. They'll check the eyes, ears, and mouth for any abnormalities. They'll listen to your dog's heart, lungs, and belly to make sure everything sounds normal. Your dog will also have their temperature taken. Also, the vet will run their hands along your dog to make sure

*Photo Courtesy of*
*Lindsey Hauser*

everything is fine with their legs, back, and belly. If your dog needs to have any further routine tests done, like a heartworm test, the vet will take your dog back to the lab and draw blood.

The reason it's so important to schedule a checkup every year is that a vet can quickly diagnose an issue you might not even notice. And, if you go regularly, they can track changes from year to year, pinpointing issues to keep an eye on. If you only go to the vet when your dog is sick, there's no benchmark to compare to your dog's healthy state. Also, if you only take your dog to the vet when you notice symptoms, your dog's condition may have been caught earlier.

# Fleas, Ticks, and Worms

Part of preventative care is taking precautions to keep parasites off of your dog. Dogs are like magnets for these parasites because they often eat things they shouldn't and wander around overgrown areas. Once the parasites latch onto your dog, it may be hard to tell that your dog has an infestation. These critters can easily grow or spread before you even notice any symptoms.

Intestinal worms are fairly common in puppies, so it's not necessarily a deal breaker if your breeder informs you about that part of your dog's medical history before you buy. However, adult dogs can acquire intestinal worms, especially if they spend time around other animals. If you notice your dog's eating habits have changed, their bowel movements are irregular, or if they're lethargic or vomiting, have a vet check them out. A stool sample can show if there are any worms in their digestive tract and medicine will care of the issue. Heartworms are another parasite, but these travel through the bloodstream, instead of the digestive system. When infected mosquitoes bite your dog, the heartworm is released into the bloodstream, eventually making its way to the heart. This parasite can be deadly if not treated immediately. Luckily, there's a monthly preventative medicine that can keep your dog protected against heartworms. After a quick blood test, your vet will prescribe a medication to give to your dog at the same time every month. As long as you give this medicine to your dog on a regular basis, you won't have to worry about heartworm. If you're late to administer the preventative and there are mosquitoes where you live, you may need to go to the vet for another test, just to be safe.

Fleas and ticks are external parasites that can easily latch onto your dog, especially if your dog spends time around other animals or likes to play outside. Luckily, it's pretty easy to spot these parasites and their markings on a Pit Bull, due to their short coat. These creatures suck the blood from your dog and can possibly pass on dangerous diseases. Plus, fleas cause extreme itchiness and are hard to kill once an infestation starts. To prevent your dog from bringing these pests home, choose a preventative that works best for your pup. Topical preventatives are liquids can be applied to your dog's coat once a month. There are also oral preventatives that cause fleas and ticks to die when they bite your dog. If fleas and ticks cannot survive on your pooch, then there's less of a chance of these pests reproducing and causing your dog harm. If you aren't sure which type of preventative to choose, talk to your vet. Your location, your pet's medical history, and your comfort in administering these preventatives all factor into this decision.

# Vaccinations

Vaccinations are essential to preventative care and some shots are even required by law. There are a handful of contagious diseases that veterinarians can vaccinate against, starting when your dog is a puppy. Not only do these vaccines keep your dog healthy, but they reduce the spread of easily preventable and devastating illnesses. Some fatal diseases, like rabies, can be transmitted to humans. In many states and countries, your dog must be up to date on their recommended vaccinations in order to take training classes or even go to dog parks. The rabies vaccine is required to license your dog because an unvaccinated dog can become a public health risk.

Vaccination is a controversial topic, but there is really no good reason not to vaccinate your dog. By keeping your dog free of contagious disease, you're doing your part in eliminating terrible viruses that kill lots of dogs. You're not only protecting your dog but other dogs who might not be up to date on their vaccines. When you get your puppy's first round of vaccinations, your vet will put your dog on a vaccination schedule, according to their age and state regulations. The clinic will then notify you every time your dog needs to get booster shots to maintain their immunity. It's an added cost to you, but it's very important that you keep your dog up to date on their shots, for the good of the canine species.

# Genetic Illnesses

As with many dogs, Pit Bulls often suffer from hip dysplasia. This is a condition that occurs when the hip socket and the ball of the femur don't create a perfect fit. Over time, this can create pain and inflammation. In serious cases, surgery may be required. You might notice symptoms of this condition if your aging dog starts limping or doesn't move as quickly as they once did. Some supplements and anti-inflammatory medications may relieve some pain, but should be prescribed by a vet.

Pit Bulls are also prone to cataracts. This is the thickening of the lens that causes cloudiness in the eye. As it progresses, your dog will begin to lose vision. This is another condition that is prevalent in old age. Surgery may correct this eye problem, or you may try to make it easier for your seeing-impaired dog to get around. If the condition progresses slowly enough, your dog may adjust to having less vision.

Yearly checkups will help your vet diagnose heart conditions. Pit Bulls are susceptible to heart rhythm irregularities and congenital defects. While this sounds concerning, many times, heart murmurs in dogs do not have a large impact on a dog's day-to-day life. However, if you notice that your dog is tiring easily, pants excessively, or is lethargic, you should take your dog in for a checkup. If problems are serious enough, medication or surgery may be needed. In most cases, however, the dog will survive with few serious issues.

Allergies are another health condition that is common in this group of breeds. Dogs can be allergic to foods, outdoor allergens, or certain chemicals. Your Pit Bull is likely most irritated by various plants found in your backyard. The symptoms your dog will probably show the most is a general itchiness. If the itching is so severe that your dog licks or scratches themselves raw, your vet might recommend an antihistamine medication or a hydrocortisone cream.

# Senior Dog Care

The average lifespan for a Pit Bull is 12–14 years, so once they reach the age of seven or so, they will be considered a senior dog. Once your dog reaches that age, he won't seem so old, so there's nothing to worry about. Dogs can have a long and healthy senior stage of their life. Senior dogs still love to play and explore, but they will slow down a little, especially compared to the energy levels they showed as a pup. Keep these changes in mind as you go about your regular routine. Eventually, you'll have to slow down a little.

Perhaps the most prevalent sign of old age is joint pain when your Pit Bull tries to walk or play. This is often noticeable when they get up the first thing in the morning or try to walk around after resting for a long period of time. There are a few things you can do to ease this stiffness and pain. For starters, make sure that your dog has a soft and supportive bed to rest on. Your young pup might have enjoyed the cool tile floor, but your old dog will probably be more comfortable on a cushy bed. If they're used to hopping up on the couch, they may have a harder time doing that as they age. If your dog lives for cuddles on the couch, you might buy a small ramp or set of stairs. There are also joint supplements that you can give your dog that will help repair some of the damage that occurs to leg joints over time. If your dog seems to be in a considerable amount of pain, talk to your vet about anti-inflammatory medication. This may be a good remedy for joint pain.

Your Pit Bull may also gain weight if they're not exercising as much as they used to. Older dogs require fewer calories than their younger counterparts. If your senior dog is gaining weight, consider reducing their daily food intake. If they have trouble eating crunchy kibble due to a dimin-

*Photo Courtesy of
Aaron Medina*

ished ability to smell or their teeth hurt when they chew, try mixing dry and wet food together to make it easier to eat. Or pour a little water or broth on top of the crunchy food. The moisture releases good smells and makes the food go down a little easier.

As your dog's joints start to age, you may change your exercise routine. While you may have been able to go on runs before, you will reach a time where that's just too much exertion for your old dog. Exercise is still important, but you may decide that an easy walk will lead to less pain and stiffness in your dog's legs. Continuing to test your dog's mental fitness with puzzles and other games is still important as they get older. It can keep their mind sharp, which will lead to less confusion and agitation. As long as your dog is still eager to go on walks and your vet hasn't told you otherwise, continue to give your dog exercise. Even if you aren't doing the same activities you once did together, your dog will still want to explore and play.

Most of all, it's important to spend quality time with your Pit Bull. These dogs are companion animals and want to snuggle up to you. You may find that as your Pit Bull ages, he's less interested in playing fetch and more interested in nestling up to you while you read a book. Cherish these moments with your dog because they won't last forever. Also, remember that dogs are considered "senior" around age seven . With proper care, it's entirely possible for your dog to live another decade from the time they're officially declared "senior."

Eventually, there will come a time where you have to say goodbye. If your dog is in a lot of pain, incontinent, or is suffering from a lot of different age-related ailments, you may decide that euthanasia is the best option. This can be extremely difficult to decide for your pet, but you'll know when your dog's condition will only get worse and their quality of life is suffering. When you're reaching this conclusion, talk to a vet for guidance. An examination can tell you if there's anything they can do for your dog. If not, they will take you through the euthanasia process.

Once you bring your dog home, you'll come to realize that there's nothing more important than ensuring your pup lives the best life he possibly can. The decisions that you make along the way have a lot to do with his health and happiness. Regular exercise, nutritious food, good hygiene, and regular veterinary visits can extend your dog's life by years, and give them lots of high-quality time with you. Remember that your veterinarian is a great resource and that you should work together to give your dog the healthcare they deserve.

A lot of people don't understand why people love their Pit Bulls, but once you bring your sweet pup home, you'll never want another breed. While these cuties have a lot of misconceptions surrounding their temperament, you'll know the truth about Pit Bulls: this breed is gentle, playful, and super sweet. They are easy to care for and make a great exercise companion. This breed is intelligent and can be trained to perform a variety of commands. It takes a lot of work to raise a dog, but at the end of the day, there's not a better companion out there than the Pit Bull!

Made in the USA
Middletown, DE
28 January 2024

48700417R00068